Rn.93

COLOUR

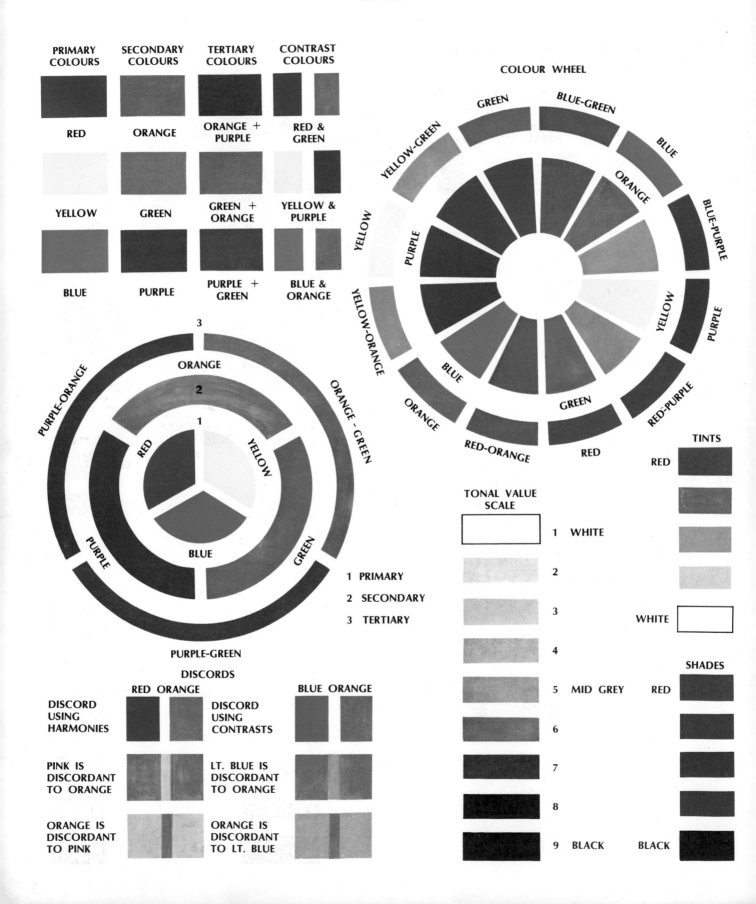

COLOUR

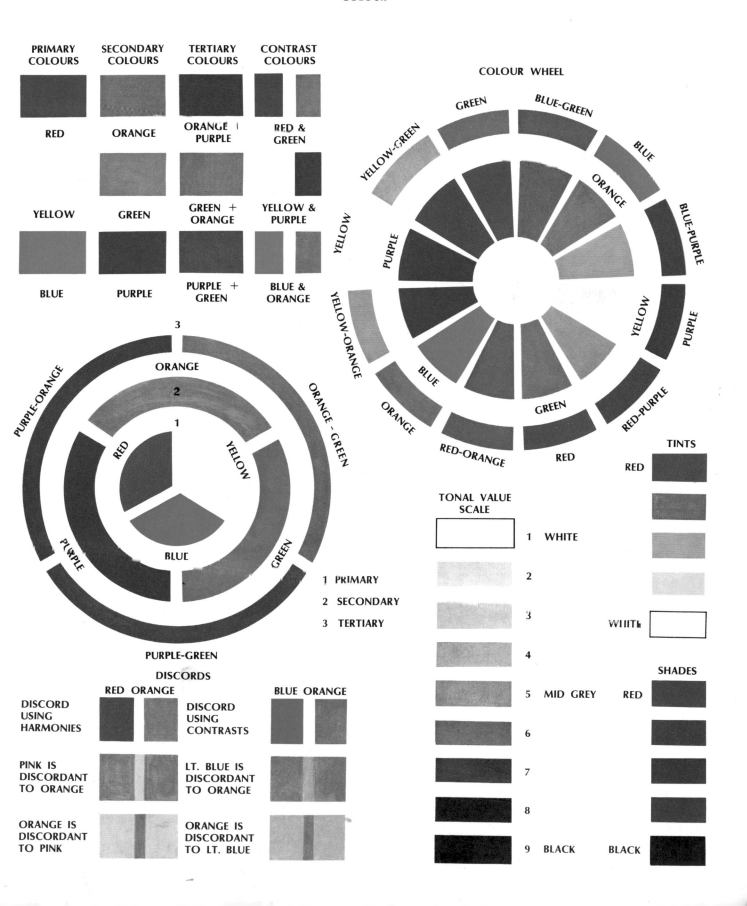

PRIMARY COLOURS
RED
YELLOW
BLUE

SECONDARY COLOURS
ORANGE
GREEN
PURPLE

TERTIARY COLOURS
ORANGE + PURPLE
GREEN + ORANGE
PURPLE + GREEN

CONTRAST COLOURS
RED & GREEN
YELLOW & PURPLE
BLUE & ORANGE

COLOUR WHEEL

GREEN
BLUE-GREEN
YELLOW-GREEN
BLUE
YELLOW
ORANGE
PURPLE
BLUE-PURPLE
YELLOW
PURPLE
BLUE
RED-PURPLE
YELLOW-ORANGE
GREEN
ORANGE
RED-ORANGE
RED

3
ORANGE
2
PURPLE-ORANGE
RED
1
YELLOW
ORANGE - GREEN
PURPLE
BLUE
GREEN
PURPLE-GREEN

1 PRIMARY
2 SECONDARY
3 TERTIARY

TONAL VALUE SCALE

1 WHITE
2
3
4
5 MID GREY
6
7
8
9 BLACK

TINTS
RED
WHITE

SHADES
RED
BLACK

DISCORDS

RED ORANGE

DISCORD USING HARMONIES

PINK IS DISCORDANT TO ORANGE

ORANGE IS DISCORDANT TO PINK

DISCORD USING CONTRASTS

LT. BLUE IS DISCORDANT TO ORANGE

ORANGE IS DISCORDANT TO LT. BLUE

BLUE ORANGE

A B C's of
FASHION & DESIGN
Gloria Mortimer-Dunn

W. FOULSHAM & Co. Ltd.
New York   Toronto   Cape Town   Sydney

W. FOULSHAM & CO. LTD.,
Yeovil Road, Slough, Bucks, England

ISBN 0-572-00872-4

Printed in Great Britain by
Lowe & Brydone (Printers) Ltd., Thetford, Norfolk.

CONTENTS

Preface vii
Careers in Fashion 1
Basic Design 2
—unity
Line 2
—harmony
—contrast
Direction 3
Shape 5
Proportion 12
Tonal Value 14
Colour 16
—harmony
—contrasts
—discord
—tonal value
Repetition 17
Gradation 19
Dominance 20
Balance 21
Texture 22
Co-ordination 23
Darts and Tucks 25
Seams and Yokes 26
Drapery 27
Front fastenings 28
Necklines 29
Collars 30
Belts and Waistlines 31
Skirts 32
Sleeves 33
Trimmings 34
Specialized detail 35
—beading
—embroidery
—lace
—quilting
Pleats 37
Frills, Flounces and Ruffles 38
Pockets and Bows 39
Textiles 40
—wool
—other animal fibres
—silk
—cotton
—linen
—other fibres
—man-made fibres
—synthetics
—inorganic fibres
—stretch fibres
—non-woven fabrics
Spinning 46

Weaving 47
—plain weave
—twill weave
—satin weave
—pattern weaves
—pile-woven fabrics
—jacquard weaves
—dobby weaves
—leno weaves
Knitting 48
—hand knitting
—machine knitting
—weft knitting
—warp knitting
—the needle
—stitches
—stitch variations
Fabric Printing 50
—block printing
—stencilling
—batik
—tie-dyeing
—discharge printing
—screen printing
—roller printing
Lace 51
—twisting
—lace types
—hand-made lace
—machine-made lace
Dyeing 54
—functional finishes
Glossary of Textile definitions 56
—summary
—fabric named
Garment definition 63
—quality
—classical garments
—fun garments
Foundation garments 64
Lingerie 65
—night wear
—house coats
Dresses 66
—cocktail wear
—dinner wear
—theatre wear
—evening wear
Coats 67
—winter coats
—summer coats
—evening coats
—capes

—rain wear

Furs   68

Suits   71

Skirts   71

Jackets   71

Blouses and Skirts   72

Knitwear   72

Ensembles   72

Separates   74

Trousers and Slacks   74

Shorts   74

Resort wear   75

Sports wear   75

   —spectator sports

   —active sports

   —water sports

   —riding

   —shooting

   —skiing

   —tennis

   —yachting

Maternity wear   78

Children's wear   79

Accessories   80

   —leather

   —belts

   —umbrellas

   —handbags

   —gloves

   —handkerchiefs

   —scarves

   —footwear

   —hosiery

   —shawls and stoles

   —jewellery

   —millinery

Haute Couture   86

Boutiques   88

Ready-to-wear   88

Mass production   89

Buyers   90

Fashion reporting   90

Garment Construction   91

   —fit

   —boning

   —padding

   —linings

   —finish

   —underlinings

   —interlinings

Planning a Basic Wardrobe   93

   —clothes for summer

   —clothes for winter

Travel   94

Luggage   94

Figure flattery   95

   —age

   —cosmetics

   —perfume

   —hair

   —posture

   —grooming

Colour flattery   99

   —personal colouring

Figure types   101

   —weight chart

   —the short figure

   —the tall figure

   —the angular figure

   —the heavy figure

   —the hip-heavy figure

   —the top-heavy figure

Face flattery   118

   —the round face

   —the long face

   —the square face

   —the heart-shaped face

   —glasses

PREFACE

Fashion developed from the need to protect the body from the weather and the desire to adorn it.

Fashion evolution has been gradual. Until early this century, wealth was displayed by rich colour and fabric, elaborate styling, and lavish trimming. The emancipation of woman's clothing came with the First World War. Vast changes were made in fashion (shorter skirts, the disappearance of whalebone) and, as life became more active, so fashion was adapted to meet the new requirements. The bias cut which was developed in the thirties introduced a new way of handling fabrics, producing a more fluid line by moulding to the shape of the body.

Years ago there were well laid down rules for fashion, such as when and where to wear hats and long gloves, and what colours and fabrics to choose to be acceptable. With the accelerated pace of living, the flood of new ideas, and the technical advance in the textile and manufacturing fields, these rules no longer apply.

Good design is pleasing to the eye and flattering to the wearer. The style, fabric, and colour should be attractive, and the cut, fit, and finish without fault. The garment should be suitable for the occasion, comfortable to wear and, above all, practical. All garments should be without unnecessary detail and trims, and worn with carefully selected accessories as everything in the design must have *purpose*. This adds up to elegant dressing.

Any fashion and colour combinations can be either vulgar or chic depending on the taste used in its creation. Today, purple, orange, and pink are used together for resort wear, whereas years ago the colour purist would have been horrified at such misuse of colour.

To adapt or modify the latest fashion trends, great care must be taken to retain the general look of the original design. Basic designs can be altered just by moving the waist or hemline up or down, varying the length of the sleeve, changing the neckline, or by adding detail such as pockets and flaps. Endless permutations can be achieved.

Fashion today has a youthful look with an easy, fluid shape that moves with the body and is elegant for, women of all ages. This look prevails in all good fashion where nothing is overstressed, the line is understated with the minimum of detail, and the fabric is in complete harmony with the garment shape.

Simplicity, good taste, and grooming are the three main fundamentals of understated elegance and good dressing.

This book will serve as a manual for all those interested in fashion design. It is divided into several sections, each dealing with a different aspect of fashion. Each section traces the basic design, colour, textiles, and requirements of each garment definition and figure type. The differences between haute couture, ready-to-wear, and mass-produced garments are described in detail.

n a particular feature
s, or welt stitching wh
n will result in a co

1945	1946	1947	1948
1951	1951	1952	1952
1954	1954	1955	1955

THICK   THIN

C

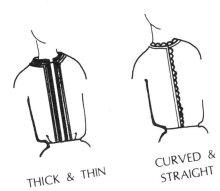

THICK & THIN   CURVED & STRAIGHT

Design as many garments as possible

DIRECTION
Lines must have direction, and are eith
zontal, (|) vertical, or (\ /) oblique

Horizontal lines are broade

CAREERS IN FASHION

Careers in fashion are many and varied, but without doubt the most interesting one is designing. Anyone can design clothes, but not everyone can be a good and successful designer. Talent and flair are required. However, taste can be cultivated, and the eye trained to not only appreciate line, texture, and colour, but also to distinguish good design from bad.

To be able to sketch is an advantage. Ideas can be refined and altered on paper without wasting time and fabric. New ideas and any interesting changes in fashion can be sketched for future reference. It is necessary for a designer to be able to make a clear diagrammatic sketch of the suggested style, indicating its shape and proportion, noting all detail, seams, darts, and trim. This is essential when the design is handed over to the sample department to prepare the pattern and cut out the garments. For those who have no natural ability in drawing, an outline sketch of a basic figure will serve as an adequate diagram on which to place the design. This diagram can be placed under a thin or transparent sheet of paper and the design drawn on the top piece of paper, using the diagram as a guide to ensure that the figure proportions are correct and to avoid distortion of design.

To be able to interpret fashion sketches from a magazine or newspaper, a basic training is essential. These sketches show only the minimum lines of the design, thus avoiding details such as seams, darts, and back views. An experienced pattern-maker is able to interpret a rough sketch, but the subtle variations in proportion, shape, and detail need the special touch of the experienced designer. Working from photographs is easier since the proportions have not been altered by artistic licence. Keen observation will help solve most of the problems encountered and supply missing detail.

A designer must always think in 3 dimensions with an eye for colour and detail, and the ability to create and adapt fashion. He must, also, have enthusiasm with a capacity for hard work as well as the ambition to succeed. In fact, a designer must be totally dedicated to fashion. It is necessary for him to watch future trends, assess with some accuracy those which will appeal to a large section of the buying public, and judge the correct time to launch them. A close study of fashion periodicals will keep him aware of the coming trends, and help predict the fashion for the coming season.

It helps to have a preliminary training in a fashion school or be apprenticed to a well-established fashion house while attending night school. This will give a sound knowledge of the profession and its limitations as well as a solid training in design and textiles, pattern making, and garment construction. A designer must be able to guide the model sample from sketch to finished garment regardless of the number of assistants he may have.

A young designer generally starts as an assistant to a head designer or assists in the sample department in a firm, and as a junior would not be expected to have great knowledge or vast experience. The basic principles learnt beforehand would be of great advantage. Other attributes needed are a strong constitution to stand the high pressure of work, commonsense, and the humour to survive.

Designers in mass-produced, ready-to-wear clothing firms are frequently only interpreters of the latest fashion styles, adapting them to public demand rather than creating original designs. The design scope is also limited but interesting in such fields as accessories, millinery, jewellery, children's wear, outsize, and maternity wear.

Until experience is gained, it is better for the designer not to enter his own business, be it a workroom or shop. Even with sufficient financial backing this must be well planned and organized efficiently to be able to cover salaries, overheads, taxes, and to make a profit.

Not everyone has the creative ability for designing, but other fields in the fashion world can be as rewarding. Whatever the field chosen, a basic knowledge of design, colour, textiles, and manufacturing is invaluable. There are many careers at all levels in the technical field; manufacturing, marketing, merchandising, retail and wholesale, fashion promotion and co-ordination, publicity, display, advertising in stores, boutiques, newspapers, or magazines. Designers are required for haute couture, wholesale, retail as well as specialized designers for the theatre, films, and television. Textile designers are required for weaving, knitting, or printing of fabrics in a design studio or textile mill. Fashion artists, graphic designers, and commercial artists are required for layout and promotion in advertising.

Remember that experience is always the best teacher, and knowledge gained in any of the fashion fields will give an excellent background to any of these careers.

BASIC DESIGN

To become a good designer, it is essenti[al]
of the relationship between the·basic
elements of design and their applicati[on]
This understanding will greatly ass[ist]
designing of all apparel and accessori[es]
The essential principles of elementar[y]
are

- line
- direction
- shape
- proportion.

Into these rudiments come

- texture
- tonal value
- colour.

Applied to all these are

- harmony
- repetition
- gradation
- contrast.

In design is found

- balance
- dominance
- co-ordination.

UNITY

Unity in design is the
principles to create goo[d]
fashion, be it clothes, tex[
styling of a dress, the bod[
the impression of being

LINE

A line can be straight,
broken, or textured.

STRA[IGHT]

1927   1928   1929

1933   1934   1935

1939   1940   1941

8

COLOUR

Colour is produced by the st[
eye.

Hue — Hue is the name o[
and character by w[
colour from anoth[
green, or orange.

Value — Value is the tonal gr[
dark colours. The q[
a dark blue from a[
value between blac[

Chroma — Chroma is the str[
purity of a colour. 1[
same hue (red), th[
lighter nor darker th[
different colour stre[ngth
a bright, clear red w[
terra-cotta.

Primary colours: blue
                      red
                      yellow

Secondary   green =
colours: orange=
                      purple =

Sub-secondary   blue-gree[n
colours: red-purpl[e
                      yellow-or[ange

Tertiary colours: orange mi[
                      green mix[
                      purple mi[

Breaking a colour by mixing [
or colours will give a wider ran[ge
pure colour, but what it gains i[
in brilliance.

Tints — White added to any c[
Shades — Black added to any co[

HARMONY

Adjoining hues on the colour v[
These colours are always pleasa[nt

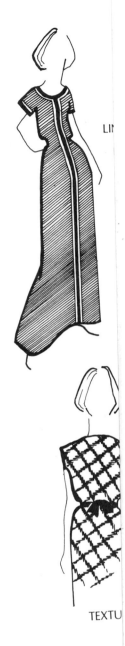

DOMINANCE

LI[

TEXTU[

Unity in design re[
direction, one shap[
sufficiently emphasiz[
and vertical lines a[
should be dominan[
lacks a point of inter[

A focal point can [
or an interesting fea[

DARTS AND TUCKS

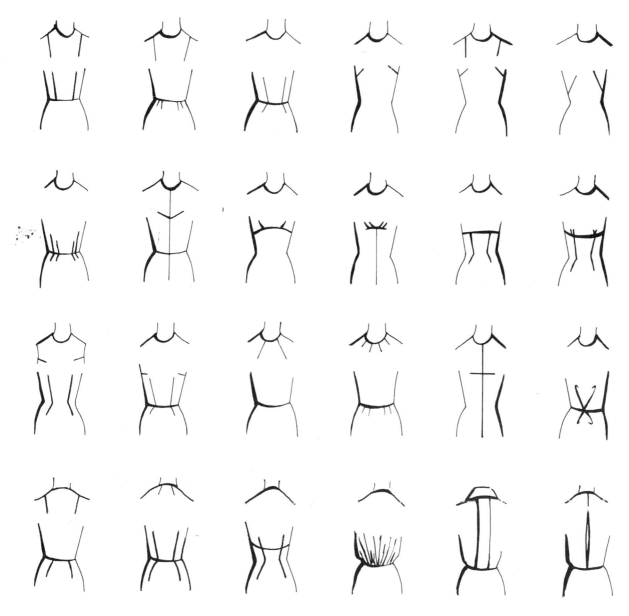

Darts are extremely important to the shape of a garment and are placed to remove fullness where it is not required. On the front bodice, the darts radiate from the bust point with the stitching starting just away from the point. Darting of the back bodice is used to shape the fabric over the shoulder blades and to the waist. On the skirt the darting is over the hips and to the waist.

Darts must always be stitched off to nothing as a bubble at the end of a badly-sewn dart is ugly. Often it is more attractive to have two small darts in a particular position than one large, bulky one.

Tucks are a softer way of eliminating superfluous fullness. In fabrics such as satin, it is frequently better to use tucks or seams instead of darts. Seams, gathers, folds, and unpressed pleats are alternative methods of shaping and fitting a garment.

SEAMS AND YOKES

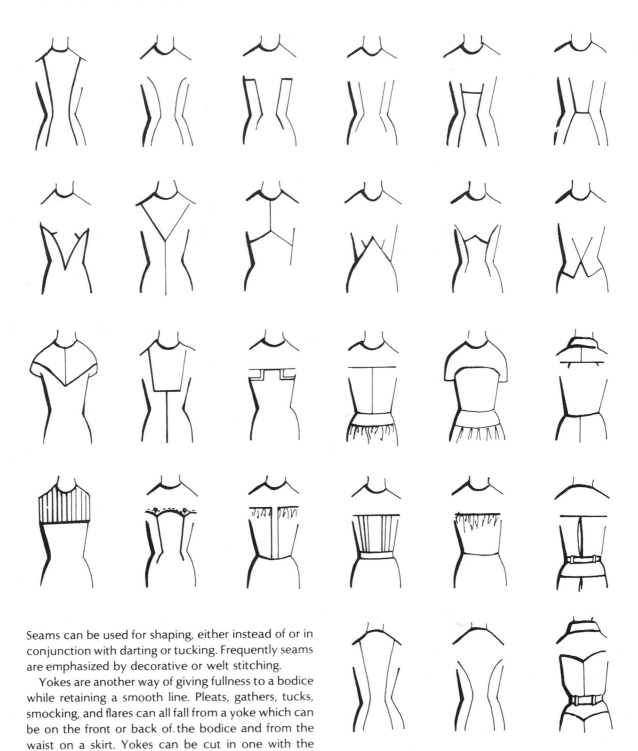

Seams can be used for shaping, either instead of or in conjunction with darting or tucking. Frequently seams are emphasized by decorative or welt stitching.

Yokes are another way of giving fullness to a bodice while retaining a smooth line. Pleats, gathers, tucks, smocking, and flares can all fall from a yoke which can be on the front or back of the bodice and from the waist on a skirt. Yokes can be cut in one with the sleeves.

DRAPERY

Garments can be fitted or moulded on the figure or a dress-stand by means of French drapery, unpressed pleats, folds, or by cutting the fabric on the bias grain. The subtle balance of folds can be altered by adjusting the fall of the fabric. This can be done by raising or lowering the folds or by adding or subtracting fabric in the drapery. Drapery can fall from one or more points and the folds can radiate from these points.

The correct type and weight of fabric is essential as it must have sufficient body to fall in fluid folds. Crepe and silk jersey fabrics are ideal, while chiffons and sheer silks have to be mounted on an underlining to retain the garment shape.

FRONT FASTENINGS

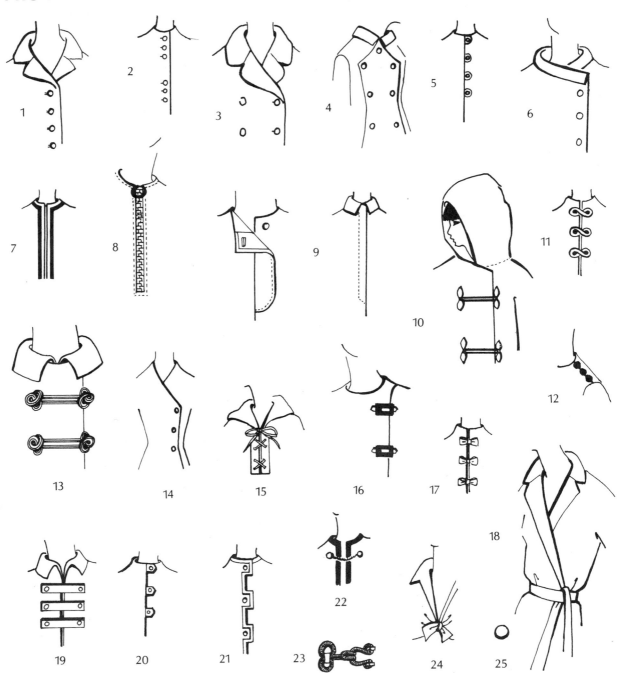

1 Single-buttoned   2 Three-button grouping
3 Double-breasted   4 Single- and double-buttoned
5 Looped   6 Side-buttoned   7 Concealed
8 Zip   9 Fly   10 Toggled   11 Braid
12 Shoulder-buttoned   13 Frogging   14 Cross-over

15 Laced-up   16 Buckled   17 Bow   18 Wrapped
and tied   19 Strap   20 Tab   21 Notched
22 Linked   23 Ornamental hook and eye
24 Knotted tie   25 Stud

NECKLINES

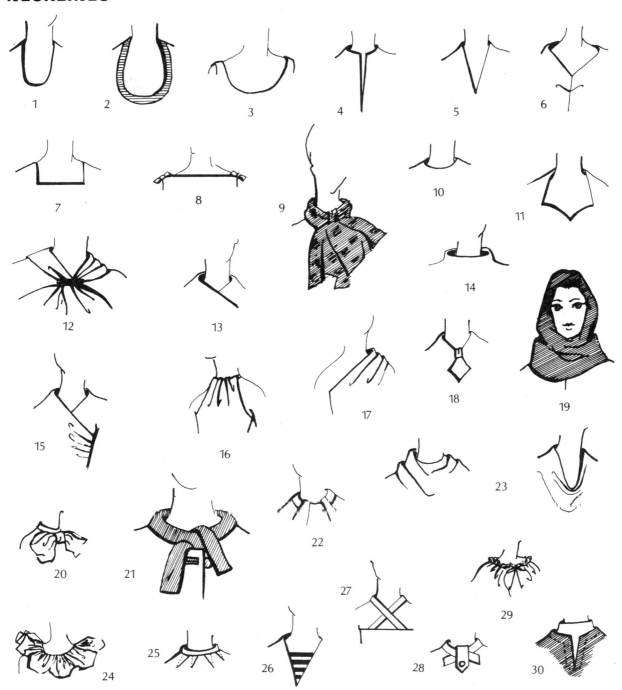

1 U-shape   2 Horseshoe   3 Scoop   4 Slot
5 Vee-neck   6 Wide Vee   7 Square   8 Bateau or boat   9 Scarf   10 Round   11 Sweetheart
12 Draped   13 Wrap   14 Stand-away
15 Cross-over   16 Halter   17 Asymmetric

18 Keyhole   19 Hooded   20 Bow   21 Tie
22 Tucked   23 High and low cowl   24 Frilled
25 Darted   26 Neck with fill-in   27 Strap
28 Tab   29 Drawstring   30 Double.

COLLARS

1 Peter Pan   2 Puritan   3 Eton   4 Prussian
5 Shawl   6 Turtle   7 Polo   8 Mandarin or Chinese
9 Bertha   10 Roll   11 Sailor   12 Knit-shirt
13 Scarf   14 Tie   15 Picture   16 Tailored

17 Button-down   18 Funnel   19 Draped   20 High
21 Peaked   22 Swallow   23 Stand-away   24 Strap
25 Coat   26 Collar with stand   27 Horseshoe
28 Stand-up   29 Milano   30 Cross-over.

BELTS AND WAISTLINES

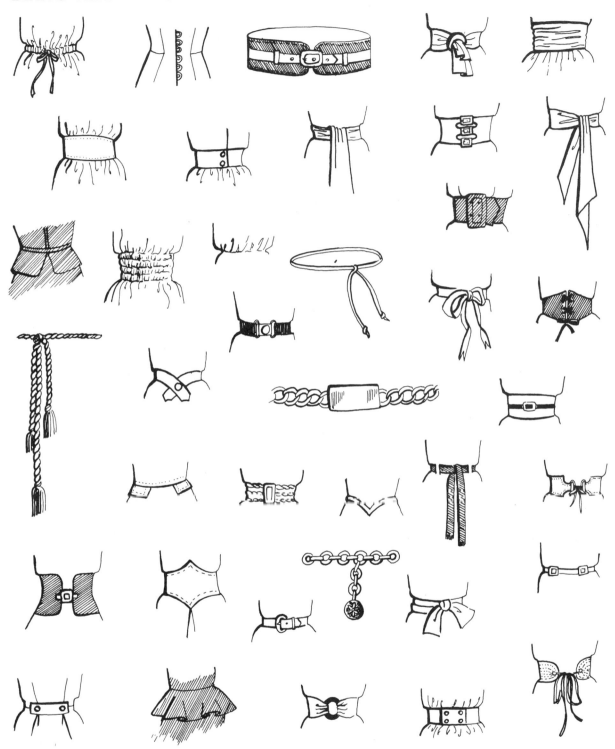

SKIRTS

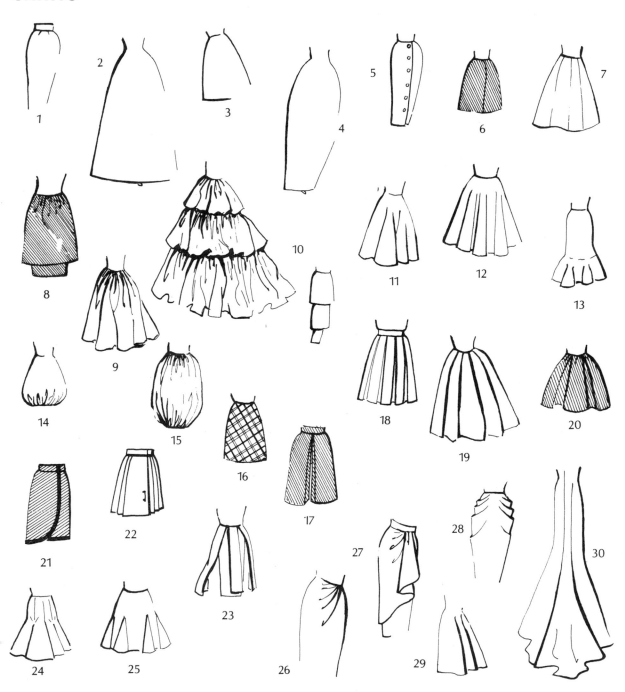

1 Straight or sheath   2 Bell   3 Flared   4 Tulip
5 Button-through   6 Four-gore   7 Eight-gore
8 Overskirt   9 Gathered   10 Tiered   11 Half-circle
12 Circle   13 Skirt with flounce   14 Harem
15 Balloon   16 Bias-cut   17 Culotte   18 Pleated
19 Unpressed pleats   20 Pleated-gore   21 Wrap
22 Kilt   23 Flying panels   24 Trumpet   25 With
godets   26 Draped   27 Side-draped   28 Peg-top
29 With back fullness   30 Fish-tail.

SLEEVES

1 Raglan   2 Saddle-shoulder   3 Cuffed
4 Two-piece   5 Edwardian puff   6 Batwing
7 Blouse   8 Bon-bon   9 Drawstring   10 Shirt
11 Frilled   12 Balloon   13 Kite   14 Puff
15 Kimono   16 Cape   17 Shirred   18 Split and tied
19 Cap   20 Tiered   21 Bishop   22 Flared
23 Lantern   24 Set-in   25 Dolman   26 Rib-knit
27 Cross-over   28 Magyar   29 Bell   30 Layer.

CAP
SHORT
ELBOW LENGTH
$\frac{3}{4}$ LENGTH
BRACELET LENGTH
LONG

33

TRIMMINGS

Trimming of any description is designed as part of a garment and never added as an afterthought. Too much trimming can spoil an otherwise attractive outfit and make it fussy and vulgar. If the ensemble is too stark, wear elegant accessories or jewellery rather than use unwise trimming.

Trimming fads change each season, but the basic fashion line alters less frequently. Leave trimming off when in doubt rather than cheapen the appearance of the outfit.

BRAIDS

Braids are added as a finishing touch or trim to a garment. Braids made of rayon impart a higher lustre than those of other fibres.

BUTTONS

Carefully selected buttons give an inexpensive garment a quality touch. Very ornamental buttons usually cheapen the garment. Buttons covered with the fabric of the dress are quite smart; other choices are wood, metal, casein, horn, plastic, jet, glass, and jewels.

FEATHERS

Feathers worn with great discrimination look glamorous; otherwise they look ridiculous. Their distinction allows them to be worn only as a feather boa or feather-trimmed hat.

FLOWERS

Indiscriminate adding of flowers, real or artificial, to an outfit designed to be without embellishments kills the intended effect.

A single flower on a suit lapel or covering a summer hat can enhance the appearance. A one-coloured evening gown worn with flowers in the hair looks well on a young girl.

Printed fabrics are the best use of flowers in chic dressing.

FRINGES

Fringes of self-fabric, wool, silk, beads, or leather stripes appear attractive on some garments and accessories.

RIBBONS

Plain or fancy ribbons in cotton, silk, rayon, or nylon in satin, faille, grosgrain, velvet, or taffeta is used mainly for evening wear, lingerie, children's wear, and millinery.

Ribbon is frequently used in conjunction with lace, to be threaded through holes provided.

SPECIALIZED DETAIL

Pleating, beading, appliqué, smocking, quilting, and embroidery are just a few of the specialized processes that require complicated and expensive equipment and skilled operators. Many manufacturers avail themselves of the services offered by outside specialists for a complete professional look to their garments.

BEADING

Beading should always be left in the hands of skilled specialists. Nothing looks worse than a few badly-placed beads stitched on a garment by an amateur seamstress. The epitome of beading is the all-over jewel-encrusted beading of an haute couture evening gown.

Single beads or pearl drops placed in the centre of lace flowers look attractive and add glamour to a gown. Frequently beading is placed heavily at the neckline, gradated to nothing at the waistline of a bodice. This form of decoration is particularly suitable for evening gowns because the front bodice is mainly on view. Beaded bands or motifs can be slip-stitched into position on a garment if not directly beaded onto the fabric.

Paillettes or sequins can be successfully done only by an expert. Only those with a slim figure should wear garments covered with paillettes; otherwise 10 pounds will be added to the look of the figure. Paillettes can be mixed with beads, pearls, and embroidery in decorating a gown.

EMBROIDERY

For gala occasions or evening wear, embroidery can be sumptuous combined with beading. Silk, wool, metal thread, and rayon are some of the yarns that can be worked into embroidery. Fabric can be embroidered with raffia, linen, or thick cotton (avoiding the "peasant" look) and used for casual wear. Restraint must be used in the choice of accessories so that they are plain and as tasteful as possible. A simple hairstyle is best worn with embroidered garments.

Hand-embroidered lingerie with scallops is still considered a luxury and is definitely more chic than heavily lace-trimmed garments.

Simple embroidery for children's wear is always popular and is often combined with appliqué. The more elaborately embroidered garments are reserved for christenings.

LACE

Beautiful lace is essentially a feminine and very dressy fabric. Except for lingerie and trimming on children's apparel, all lace garments look more elegant when worn after dark.

Lightly embroidered lace patterns with a sheer mesh background, such as Chantilly, require a fine net for underlining to add body to the fragile fabric. The sleeves can be left unlined for a more transparent effect. The net underlining is cut and made with the fabric. The heavier laces such as guipure and Cluny may be underlined for an opaque look or worn over a strapless slip. The haute couture way to handle seams is to overlap the edges and applique the lace together, using the dominant design of the lace pattern as a seam line. The surplus lace is then trimmed away, leaving an almost invisible seam.

Great care must be taken in the choosing of accessories and jewellery so that they enhance a lace garment and do not make it appear cheap and vulgar. All trimming must be restrained to avoid giving an overdressed appearance.

QUILTING

Quilting is used primarily for additional warmth. Wadding, either of cotton or synthetic fibres, is sandwiched between two fabrics which are held together by stitching. This stitching raises or gives lift to the design. The patterns used for quilting vary from the simple traditional diamond design to more intricate patterns which include embroidery.

Quilting is used in anoraks, parkas. and for lining in winter coats because it is recognized as an insulator against the cold.

1 Shirring   2 Rouleau   3 Cording   4 Pin tucks
5 Embroidery   6 Quilting with bound edges
7 Beading   8 Piping   9 Smocking   10 Appliqué.

PLEATS

1 KNIFE   2 TUCK   3 EDGE-STITCH   4 FLAT   5 DOUBLE   6 SIDE
7 PART   8 ACCORDION   9 SUNRAY   10 BOX   11 KICK   12 HEM
13 SINGLE-INVERTED   14 UNPRESSED

Pleats are very feminine and add grace to a garment by their swinging movement.
They allow for fullness without bulk and are slimmer than gathers. Pleats are versatile.
They can be very fine, all-over, or single-inverted.

FRILLS, FLOUNCES, AND RUFFLES

1 Cascade 2 Ascot 3 Ruffle 4 Double frill 5 Waterfall
6 Tiered flounce 7 Pleated frill 8 Bound-edge frill 9 Jabot
10 Pie frill 11 Stand-up frill 12 Ruff 13 Double ruffle
14 Flounce

POCKETS AND BOWS

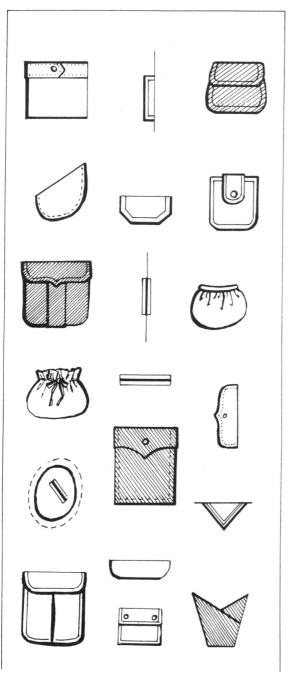

Frequently ornamental, pockets add interest to a design. Functional pockets must be placed at a practical angle for easy access.

The most feminine of trimming details, bows can be tailored or soft, functional or ornamental. Bows must be carefully placed on a garment or the outfit will appear fussy and overtrimmed.

TEXTILES

It is essential for a designer to know the basic principles and characteristics of fabrics and to be able to distinguish between the different weaves and knits. A knowledge of printing and dyeing techniques is also of great value. This knowledge need not be of a highly technical nature but sufficient to assist in selecting the best fabric for the design.

The term *textile* now covers any fabric that has been woven, knitted, crocheted, bonded, felted, or prepared in any way.

Most fabrics are manufactured with fibres twisted or spun together to form long strands called yarn, which is woven or knitted to produce the finished fabric. Thickness or number of fibres, the degree of twist and texture of yarn, and variations in weave or knit bring about endless variety in the final product. The exceptions are non-wovens, felt, and plastic.

Early this century, man-made fibre (rayon) entered the textile world, albeit at the cheap end of the trade. Only during the Second World War were any great steps taken to improve the man-made or synthetic fabrics. Once fabric was typed: silk for the wealthy upper class, wool for the middle class, and cotton for the poor. Advanced technology and imagination lifted cotton out of the kitchen and into the ballroom.

Time spent on selecting the most suitable fabric for a particular design is never wasted. Without a close relationship between the fabric and the design, the desired effect cannot be achieved. This is apparent when one fabric has been substituted for another during manufacture of a garment. If the second fabric has not the same or similar characteristics of weight, handle, and construction, it is impossible to achieve the same results. Colour blending and surface interest used in connection with the correct fabric will give eye appeal to a good design.

Complicated designs call for plainer fabric, whilst a simple design can take a luxurious fabric such as brocade or lace. The easiest fabrics to handle are cotton, linen, and fine wool. In fact, all natural fibres have excellent feel or handle while lace, chiffon, satin, and velvet require expert handling to do justice to them. Fashion in prints changes frequently with demure little pastel-coloured prints one year, followed possibly by large, brightly coloured abstract designs or monotones.

Fabrics are the raw materials of fashion.

WOOL

Wool is ideal for all occasions because it handles superbly. With modern treatment and finishes, most wool can now be washed without shrinkage. The natural properties of wool make it easy to handle; it can be shaped, moulded, and shrunk into the desired shape by steam-pressing. Wool is a natural protein hair fibre from the fleece of sheep. The best wool is found on sheep which have been specially and consistently bred for yielding wool. Different types of sheep supply fine, medium, long, and cross-bred wool.

Virgin wool is new wool which has never been processed. Re-processed wool is made from wool scraps and fibres that have been knitted, woven, or felted; although these have never been used, they are reduced to fibre state again and re-processed. Re-used wool has been used, reduced to fibre state, and re-processed.

Woollen fabrics are made from yarns more loosely twisted than worsted yarns. The short protruding fibres give a fuzzy appearance to the fabric, which can be napped if desired. The long, combed fibres of worsted yarn are tightly twisted to give a smooth, strong yarn ideal for tightly woven, firm fabric most suitable for quality suitings. Knitted fabrics can be constructed of either woollen or worsted yarn depending on the type of knit required.

Wool fibre has many characteristics which make it an excellent fibre for garments.

Crimp:	Wool fibre grows in a wavy form with a certain amount of twist. Generally the finer the count, the greater the number of crimps.
Absorption:	Wool fibre can absorb up to 20% of its weight without feeling damp, and up to 50% from other moisture, such as rain and snow.
Felting:	Felting is the ability of wool fibres to contact and interlock when exposed to moisture, heat, or pressure.
Insulation:	The construction of wool gives the fibres insulation quality. Wool is a non-conductor of heat or cold. The tiny air pockets created by the surface of the fabric retain the air and provide insulation.

in the term "gauge," which refers to the number of needles or wales per inch.

WEFT KNITTING

In circular knitting, the needles are set in round beds which rotate in a cylinder producing a tubular fabric. Flat-bed machines are those in which the needles are placed in a straight line on long, flat needle beds. Basic machines for weft knitting are:

    plain circular
    rib circular
    circular links-and-links
    basic flat-bed machine
    links-and-links flat-bed.

WARP KNITTING

Fabrics constructed by knitting yarns fed from a warp beam are called warp-knitted fabrics and the type of stitch used is called a warp stitch, which has many variations.

Warp-knitted fabrics are constructed on special flat-bed warp-knitted machines which give a flat selvedge. There are many different types of machines which knit numerous varieties of design and texture, some knitted to resemble tightly woven fabrics and others so loosely constructed as to be similar to lace. Warp knits have less give and more firmness than others.

The best known warp knits are:

    one-bar tricot —resembles the plain stitch in
                     weft knitting
    two-bar tricot —fine lines on the surface of the
                     fabric with cross-ribbed back
    milanese stitch—fine twill rib on both surfaces of
                     the fabric
    raschel stitch —There is no distinct raschel
                     stitch as there are so many

PLAIN STITCH   PURL STITCH   1 x 1 RIB STITC

THE NEEDLE

The knitting n
knitting mach
The two types
needle used f
yarns, and the

STITCHES

Most patterns
nation of the
warp.

PLAIN STITCH
Fabrics knitte
chain-like stitc
face to the fa
stitches give a
also termed je

This stitch
stitch is broke
vertical or wa

PURL STITCH
Fabric knitted
sides of the f
wrong side of
stitch can only
which can be
quite elastic
ways.

RIB STITCH
Rib stitch is co
needles knitti

---

methods have
them. Fabrics m
water-carried sp
because less wat
free of wrinkles.

All synthetic f
pressed with a
soften and disto
point. The high
give a smooth, s
on squeezing. Sy
to damage fro
bacteria, and ot

POLYMIDE (nylc
The advent of r
transformed all
habits of million
were as quick t
rayon or "art silk

Nylon is stron
easier to dye tha
can be warm or
of the fabric. Th
forced through
solidify on coolir
facture of rayon
or multifilament
as required. Spu

POLYESTER (Tery
The method of
of nylon, altho
different. It can b
or spun into yar

ACRYLICS
Acrylics are usua
fibres. This staple
fluffy yarn which
produces light,
Acrylic yarns car
a firm fabric. Th
nylon, although

INORGANIC FIB
GLASS, MINERAL
An important po
non-tarnishable
which can be wa
yarns are general

COTTON

Cotton is the most versatile of natur
through different twist weaves and fini
an endless variety of fabrics. Cotton
vegetable fibre from the pod of a plar
"seed hair" because of the fluffy fibres
the seeds of the cotton boll. The very sl
known as linters or cotton lint. Ideal for s
cotton in its natural state is a good cond
allowing the heat to pass quickly from th

Sea Island cotton is the finest, with a l
handle. It has the longest of all fibre sta
from 1½ inches to 2½ inches in length. Egy
has lustre and a high tensile strength. U
most extensively cultivated of all cotton.
other cotton species are Prima, Peruvian,
Indian.

THE FIBRE

There are two types of cotton yarn—
combed. Carded yarn is produced from
and usually is a coarser, thicker yarn.
expensive combed cotton is from the lon;
is usually more tightly twisted.

Pick: to machine-harvest the
                pods or cotton bolls
Gin: to separate the fibres or li
                cotton seeds
Open & clean: to separate the fibres and
                foreign matter
Blend: to mix the different fibres
Card: to open up the fibre and r
                dirt and the shortest fibres
                are partly straightened to
                continuous strand called a
Comb: to remove the short fibres a
                long fibres parallel for ben
                cotton yarn.
Draw & double: to lay the fibres parallel, do
                draw out the sliver
Rove: to further draw-out and
                slivers
Spin: to twist the roving into yarr
                correct amount of twist and
                required

FABRIC CONSTRUCTION

Weaving, knitting, twisting, braiding, knottin;

GENERAL FINISHES

Singe: to burn off protruding surfac

Shear: to cut the fleece from the sheep
Class: to sort the fleece into graded qualities
Scour: to remove the natural grease and dirt
Card: to eliminate burrs and other foreign
             matter and partly lay the fibres
             parallel
Comb & gill: to comb out the short fibres and lay
             the remaining fibres parallel (worsteds
             only, to obtain a smoother yarn)
Draw & double: to further straighten the parallel fibres
             and draw into a sliver
Rove: to slightly twist the sliver into a rove.
Spin: to twist the roving into yarn (woollen
             fabrics require a soft, loosely spun
             yarn and worsted need a smooth,
             highly twisted yarn)

FABRIC CONSTRUCTION

Weaving, knitting, twisting, or felting.

FINISHES

Preparatory Treatments

Burr: to inspect and mend the knots of
             yarn in the fabric
Scour: to clean out all foreign substances
Carbonize: to remove vegetable fibres by burning

Wet Finishes

Singe: to burn off loose fibres and lint
Crab: to set the warp and filling threads in
             the weave
Nap & gig: to raise the nap or to form a deep
             pile as desired
Wet decate: to set the pile and lustre prior to
             dyeing
Shrink: to reduce the fabric in length and
             width
Bleach: to whiten and prepare the fabric for
             dyeing or printing
Dye or print: to colour the fabric

Dry Finishes

Tender: to stretch, straighten, and dry the
             fabric
Shear: to shear off protruding fibres
Brush: to remove the short fibres
Press: to smooth the fabric and remove the
             wrinkles
Steam: to shrink the fabric
Dry decate: to set the width and length of the
             fabric and add lustre to the surface

OTHER ANIMAL FIBRES

There are many fine animal fibres which have the properties and qualities of wool and are produced commercially. Luxury fabrics constructed from these fibres have a soft, warm handle without weight.

ALPACA AND LLAMA

These animals come from South America and have strong, silky hair fibre. The lovely natural colours, varying from white to brown and black, are often blended together in yarn.

ANGORA

The hair is clipped from the angora rabbit and blended with other fibres before spinning. Rabbit hair dyes lighter than the other fibres with which it is mixed, and this gives a two-toned appearance.

CAMEL

Camel hair is strong, smooth, and lustrous, with the most valuable short hair close to the skin. The coarser outer hair is used mainly for rugs. Camel hair is a non-conductor of heat and cold, naturally water-repellent and therefore excellent for overcoats. The extreme fineness of the fibre entraps more air and so retains the body heat longer than wool.

MOHAIR

Mohair comes from the Angora goat, originally raised around Angora, a city and province of Asia Minor. The fibre is soft with a silk-like lustre and, being stronger than wool, is more durable. Mohair dyes well and retains its colour.

CASHMERE

Cashmere is the soft underhair of the cashmere goat combed out during the shedding season. The very fine fibres are softer and lighter than wool, but not as strong.

VICUNA

Vicuna is the finest, softest, and most delicate of all animal fibres, taken from a rare, wild animal which lives high in the Andes. It makes the world's most exquisite and expensive fabric.

SILK

Silk is the most luxurious animal fibre. It is stronger and longer in filament than other natural fibres. Silk is a very resilient natural protein fibre and, like wool, being a non-conductor of heat is warm to wear. The metallic content in "weighted" silk makes the fabric cooler and suitable for summer wear. The character-istics of silk are its lightness, strength, elasticity, and

absorption, as well as its
colours easily. The high lus
of colour has not been co
synthetics or other natur
China.

THE FIBRE
Raw or "thrown" silk is o
domestic mulberry silkwo
silk filament ranging from
yards in length is reeled fro
silk is mostly white or yell
smooth, lustrous, and cool
has not been weighted dur
and more expensive than c

Wild silk or tussah (tussor
of the wild silkworm which
filaments are coarser and m
and give a more textured s
silk is usually left in its natur
from shades of natural to b

Spun or "waste" silk is pr
obtained from damaged coc
beginning and end of coc
which is spun into yarn. Spu
lustrous than raw silk, but
handle. This yarn is particula
napped fabrics (such as vel
used extensively for shantun

YARN
There are two types of yarn
filaments reeled from cocoon
The yarn spun from the short

Raw Silk Filaments
The silkworm is the larva of a
hatched the caterpillars whic
air is circulated to suffocate
cocoon and dry out any
process protects the filament.
fully sorted as only perfect
reeling. The others are used for
natural gum or sericin secreti
the skeins are soaked in a
removal of the sericin or degu
can take place either before
knitting. Throwing is the twisti
filaments into yarns prior to w

Spun Silk
Unlike raw silk filaments, the s

Velvet has a woven-in pile and terry has woven-in
loops on one or both sides of the fabric.

JACQUARD WEAVES
A Jacquard loom is used for the weaving of intricate
brocades, damasks, and large designs. It is capable of
weaving plains, twill, satin, and combinations of these
weaves.

The design for Jacquard weaving is drawn on graph
paper and with chosen colours, transferred to special
pattern punch cards with a card for every filling or
weft yarn used in a repeat. The Jacquard cards are
laced together in order and mounted on the loom to
form a continuous repeat.

The individual warp threads are controlled by
means of special hooks which raise and lower the
warp ends as required by the set pattern.

DOBBY WEAVES
For small designs with a limited repeat, a dobby
attachment may be attached to a harness loom.

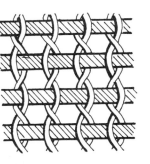

HALF-LENO WEAVE

KNITTING
Knitting is the interlooping of yarn to form a succession
of loops, each row being drawn through another to
construct a fabric. Two loops together are called a
stitch.

HAND KNITTING
Hand knitting, which is essentially a home craft, is
produced on long, hookless needles to a great variety
of patterns by the hand-manipulation of yarn.

MACHINE KNITTING
The majority of knitted fabrics are constructed on a
variety of knitting machines. Fabrics can be knitted
tubular or flat as either continuous-length "yard

HAND-MADE LACE

Needlepoint lace:	The characteristic design of needlepoint lace is a ground of net or bars which is worked with a single thread in a needle.	
Bobbin lace:	Hand-made bobbin lace is made with the design on stiff paper placed on a special lace pillow or cushion. The numerous bobbins are filled with thread which is twisted, crossed, braided, and pinned as required to reproduce the design. Bobbin lace is finer and more sheer than needlepoint lace.	
Crochet lace:	A long needle with a hook on one end to loop and twine the thread in and out is used to give the required pattern. By varying the size of the crochet hook and the thickness of the thread, crochet laces can be made fine or coarse. Crochet lace is coarser than needlepoint or bobbin lace.	
Drawn work:	Certain threads in the fabric are removed and the open space filled with lace stitches.	
Cut work:	Cut work is the term used when pieces of the fabric are cut away, the edges embroidered, and the spaces filled with lace stitches.	
Appliqué:	Lace may have motifs sewn on later. This is called appliqué.	

MACHINE-MADE LACE
Machine lace can be made on various types of
machines which differ in their bobbin construction.

Levers machine:	the first commercially efficient lace machine, using a special loom with a Jacquard system.
Nottingham machine:	used principally for coarse lace construction.
Schiffli machine:	several hundred needles controlled by a Jacquard card system to produce intricate embroideries and appliqués. (It must have a ground fabric on which to work.)
Bobbinet machine:	makes mainly net to produce a hexagonal mesh, used as a base for appliqué work or, with Jacquard attachments, to make laces.
Barmen machine:	makes certain kinds of coarse lace such as Cluny which have a plaited characteristic.
Cornely machine:	makes lock stitches and mostly used to put cordonnet on lace (particularly Alençon lace) or cord embroidered fabrics.

Below is an outline of some of the most popular laces. Originally hand laces, the characteristics are now copied by
machines.

LACE NAME	HAND LACE	MACHINE LACE	CHARACTERISTICS
Alençon	Needlepoint	Levers	Floral design heavily outlined with a cord on a very fine hexagonal mesh background.
Breton	Hand-embroidered	Schiffli	The design is embroidered on net either by hand or by machine, and the distinguishing feature is the large embroidery stitches.

Carrickmacross	Appliqué	Appliqué or Bobbinet	Fine batiste is sewn on the net with a cordonnet. The surplus batiste is cut away, leaving the net background. The design can be first cut out and then buttonholed onto the net. Rose and shamrock is the most popular design.
Chantilly	Bobbin lace	Levers	Very fine ground with a distinctive design of flowers, branches, and scrolls. Outlined by cordonnet which can be of different types of yarn. The edge has a definite scallop, and the openwork design is most pronounced. Chantilly is one of the most elaborate lace designs.
Cluny	Bobbin lace	Nottingham, Levers, or Bobbinet	A coarse, open lace with a corded appearance with a background filled with up-and-down bars. Distinct scalloped edge on the lace, which has a fabric-like texture. Wheatsheath design most popular.
Filet	Needlepoint	Nottingham, Levers, or Bobbinet	Hand-made filet has a geometric pattern darned on a knotted, square mesh. Machine filet has a square mesh filled in to form the design. Scalloped edge finished with buttonhole stitch.
Irish crochet	Crochet	Levers or Schiffli	Coarse lace with a square-mesh ground with or without picots. Rose and leaves usual design.
Mechlin	Bobbin lace	Levers	Dainty floral design with a heavy cordonnet on a very fine mesh with an open and sheer background. Lace is usually finished with a picot edge.
Milan or Guipure	Bobbin lace	Levers	Distinguished by a tape effect, making the design form a ground with an open mesh. The lace can be made by machine, with the tape forming the pattern and button-hole stitches filling in the background with bars.
Nottingham	—	Nottingham	Mosaic tile effect with a V-twist design. The lace is woven in very wide widths.
Point d'esprit	—	Levers or Bobbinet	Distinguished by a solid dot on a net background.
Point de Paris	Bobbin lace	Levers	A dainty but conspicuous pattern on a light, open mesh. The design can be either floral or geometric.
Point de Venice	Needlepoint or Crochet	Schiffli	A firm, stiff lace with a floral design made entirely by buttonhole stitch set on an open mesh.
Richelieu	Needlepoint	Schiffli	Design usually of flowers and leaves formed by button-hole stitches set on a very open mesh.

Tenerife	Bobbin lace	Levers or Barmen	The distinct wheel pattern is frequently held together by only a connection or a very open mesh.
Torchon	Bobbin lace	Levers or Barmen	A small, fan-like design made of twisted yarns with a deep scallop edge. The background is small.
Tulle	—	Levers or Bobbinet	Fine, open net with a diamond-shaped mesh.
Valenciennes	Bobbin lace	Levers or Barmen	Usually floral design on a fine mesh background with round or oval spots. Edge finished with picots or very small scallops. Valenciennes is the most widely used lace, from both beauty and price.

DYEING

Raw fibres, yarns, and fabrics may be impregnated with a colouring substance known as a dyestuff. Until the manufacture of artificial dyestuffs, fabrics were coloured by dyes extracted from products of nature—such as berries, roots, leaves, barks, and mosses.

The better known sources for natural dyes are below.

NAME	COLOUR	SOURCE
Cochineal	red	extracted from a female insect which feeds on certain cacti
Indigo	blue	extracted from the leaves of a plant
Kermes	red	obtained from a wingless female insect found in the leaves of the kermes oak
Lichen	green	obtained from mosses
Logwood	black	wood from a native American tree
Madder	red	dyestuff taken from the root of the madder herb
Saffron	yellow	flower of a plant from the crocus family.
Sepia	brown	ink from cuttlefish
Tyrian	purple	from types of shellfish or sea snails (This colour is referred to as "royal purple" because the expensive dye was for the very wealthy only.)
Woad	blue	extracted from a plant

Logwood is the only natural dye still used commercially for cheap, black dye.

PREPARATION FOR DYEING
All yarn or fabric must be prepared for dyeing by removal of all impurities like natural oils, resins, dirt, and vegetable matter. It is then dried and ready for dyeing or bleaching.

If a pure white or a pastel colour is desired, the fabric or yarn is bleached by certain chemicals to eliminate any impurities which may remain after scouring or boiling. Where a pastel colour is required, the bleached white fabric is dyed the correct shade. Prior to dyeing, a mordant chemical is applied to certain fibres to increase their acceptability to dyes.

METHODS OF DYEING
Yarn Dyed
Most textile yarns may be dyed prior to construction for greater penetration. The colour is richer and more uniform in a yarn-dyed fabric than in fabric which has been dyed after weaving or knitting. The method of dyeing raw fibres is referred to as "dyed in the wool," as the fibres are dyed before construction to give a very fast colour. After carding or combing, the fibre is dyed in the sliver or slub prior to spinning. Some fibres require a mordant bath to be able to receive the dye successfully.
Beam Dyeing
Beam dyeing is a method of warp-dyeing yarn before weaving. Dyes are forced through perforations in the beam, thus saturating the yarn with the colour.

Space-Dyed Yarn

Space-dyed yarn is dyed with multi-coloured spaces or in a single colour along a given lineal length of yarn. Space-dyeing can be repeated at even intervals or applied at random for various effects.

Piece-Dyed Fabric

The advantage of this method is that woven and knitted fabrics can be stored in the natural or grey state after construction and piece-dyed to colours as required. This economical method avoids holding large stock of unfashionable colours.

Cross-Dyeing

Cross-dyeing is the process of dyeing yarn or fabric composed of different types of fibres. The dye may colour one fibre only and leave the other either undyed or coloured to a lesser degree. The undyed fibre can be dyed another colour if required. The latest in this field are the dye-variant yarns which take on multi-colours in the one dye-bath. The secret is the different dye-uptake of the various types of nylon and terylene yarns used together in a woven or knitted fabric.

DYES

The correct dyes must be chosen for their dyeing properties and suitability to the particular fibres. Dyes differ in effectiveness with different fibres and in their reaction to sunlight, seawater, perspiration, and washing or cleaning agents. The more common classifications for dyes are as follows.

Acid Dyes

Acid dyes are commonly used on wool, other animal fibres, and nylon.

Basic Dyes

Basic dyes produce brilliant colours but have a poor resistance to light and washing. These dyes have the best affinity with wool and silk.

Direct or Commercial Dyes

Direct dyes are inexpensive and give a wide range of colours to most fibres. These are not as brilliant as acid dyes, and have a varied degree of fastness.

Mordant or Chrome Dyes

Mordant dyes are excellent for animal fibres. The colours have a high degree of fastness and are less brilliant than acid dyes. Chrome salt is the most commonly used mordant for chemically pre-treating the raw fibre.

Sulphur Dyes

Sulphur dyes are excellent dyes for vegetable fibres, rayon yarns, and fabrics. Although dull, the colours have a remarkable degree of fastness against washing.

Vat Dyes

Vat dyes can be used on most fibres and produce the clearest, brightest colours with the most resistance to washing and sunlight.

Pigment Dyes

The use of pigment dyes is most applicable to cotton, man-made, and synthetic fibres. They give a uniform colour which has an excellent degree of fastness against sunlight, washing, acids, and alkalis.

Acetate Dyes

Cellulose acetate and viscose rayons are chemically different from other textile fibres, so generally require a different group of dyestuffs.

Developed or Diazotized Dyes

Developed dyes reproduce a more satisfactory colour with excellent resistance to washing and sunlight. They are frequently used for cross-dyeing and for discharge printing.

Azoic Dyes

Azoic or naphthol dyes are excelled only by vat dyes in their degree of fastness to sunlight and washing. These dyes are frequently used to dye yarn.

FUNCTIONAL FINISHES

There are additional finishes given to fabrics to make them more suitable for a specific purpose. Depending on the type of treatment required, functional finishes may be applied at various stages during processing. Most of these finishes are durable for the life of the fabric, others are semidurable. This must be taken into consideration when choosing fabrics with certain finishes.

EMBOSSED FINISH

An embossed or crepe effect is given to the surface of the fabric by an engraved calender. The result is a lustrous pattern on a dull ground.

MOIRE FINISH

The moire finish gives a watermarked effect, especially on corded silk. The pattern is permanent on acetate, and is produced by passing the fabric through a chasing calender machine.

BONDED FINISH

Bonding is used to give additional body to a fabric. It provides insulation, controls stability to knitted, open-weave, or lace fabrics, and assists in shape retention of the garment. The bonding of knitted or woven fabrics is processed on specially designed machinery which controls the fabric tension, applies the bonding medium, presses the fabric together, and sets or cures the bond.

The fusion or foam-flame method bonds a fine layer of polyurethane foam between two fabrics. At high temperature, the foam is burnt on each side and, while tacky, is passed between two fabrics and pressed together through rollers. The foam can be applied to a single layer of fabric if required.

Another method is to spray a wet chemical adhesive onto the fabric and, by means of heat and roller application, to bond the two fabrics together.

WATERPROOF FINISH

The end use of the fabric determines whether the process should be waterproof or water-repellent. A fabric may be naturally water-resistant because of its construction or because its fibres repel water. Other fabrics have to be treated to make this possible. Many of these waterproof and water-repellent finishes alone or combined with other finishes make the fabric grease-, dirt-, and stain-resistant and impervious to mildew, perspiration, and moths.

A single- or double-sided waterproof coating applied to fabrics will make it non-porous and completely waterproof. Air vents must be added to the garment to allow for air circulation.

A water-repellent finish is applied to individual fibres, making it difficult for the water to seep through the fabric while still remaining porous. Water-repellent fabric will withstand a light shower of rain without water penetration.

CREASE-RESISTANT FINISH

To render a fabric crease- and crush-resistant, the fibres are impregnated with a resin finish. These finishes can be applied to all types of fibres and are used very successfully on linens, spun rayon, and cottons. This finish also helps retain a like-new appearance while it improves the handle and body of the fabric.

GLAZED FINISH

Synthetic resins are "baked" into the fibres at high temperature to give a durable finish to the fabric. The smooth and very highly lustrous surface resists soiling.

STARCHLESS FINISH

Obviating the use of starch in a fabric gives a crisp, smooth handle and prevents sagging after washing.

ABSORBENT FINISH

A chemically-treated finish to enable fabrics to absorb water more readily is generally used for underwear, sportswear, and terry towelling.

MOTHPROOF FINISH

Wool fabrics can be stored without precautionary measures after mothproofing. Some finishes can be washed or dry-cleaned, depending only on the end use of the fabric.

MILDEW-RESISTANT FINISH

Particularly useful for fabrics used in a hot climate, this treatment does not alter the fabric in any way, and may also be perspiration-resistant.

FIREPROOF FINISH

Fireproof fabric may char but not burn on contact with fire. The finish is an essential treatment for children's night attire.

GLOSSARY OF TEXTILE DEFINITIONS

NAME	CONSTRUCTION	APPEARANCE	GENERAL USES *	W	C	R	S	L	O
Alpaca	plain weave	firm fabric with slight lustre	coats and suits	x					
Barathea	rib or twill	fine with firm, pebbly surface	coats, suits and dresses	x	x	x	x		

* W = Wool   C = Cotton   R = Rayon   S = Silk   L = Linen   O = Other fibres or blends

				W	C	R	S	L	O
Batiste	plain weave	fine, lightweight sheer	lingerie, blouses and children's wear	x	x	x	x	x	x
Bedford cord	Bedford cord weave	medium to heavy firm fabric with lengthways ribs	sports and casual wear suits and coats	x	x	x	x		
Bengaline	rib weave	firm, closely woven, ribbed surface	dresses, suits and coats	x	x	x	x		
Bird's-eye	bird's-eye weave	soft, loose construction with a spot in the centre of each diamond	sports and casual wear		x	x		x	
Bouclé	any knit or weave	bouclé yarn used to give small, irregular surface loops	dresses, coats and suits, casual wear	x	x	x	x	x	x
Broadcloth	twill, rib, or plain weave	term covers several dissimilar fabrics	dresses, coats and suits		x	x	x		
Brocade	Jacquard weave	richly patterned with a slightly raised surface	late afternoon, evening wear		x	x	x		
Calico	plain weave	coarse, lightweight weave (often used unbleached)	printed for casual wear		x				
Cambric	plain weave	fine, lightweight, firm fabric with a soft lustre	dresses, lingerie and children's wear		x		x		
Camel hair	twill or plain weave	heavy fabric with pile surface	suits and coats						x
Cashmere	woven or knitted	very soft, lustrous fibre used alone or blended with other fibres	knitwear, dresses and coats						x
Cavalry twill	twill weave	medium to heavy weight, firm, hard surface	sports and casual wear	x					x
Chambray	plain weave	soft, fine, closely woven fabric with lustrous frosted appearance	dresses, blouses and sports wear		x			x	
Chenille	plain weave or knits	Chenille yarn used to form a pile surface	knitwear and casual wear and trimming	x	x	x			
Cheviot	herringbone or twill weave	medium to heavy weight from shaggy, coarse yarn	coats and suits	x	x	x			
Chiffon	plain weave	lightweight, open-weave gossamer sheer from high-twisted yarns	evening wear, blouses, dresses and scarves	x		x	x		
Chintz	plain weave	printed fabric with a full or semi-glazed surface	sports wear and dresses, children's wear		x				

				W	C	R	S	L	O
Corduroy	corduroy weave	raised, cut pile with vertical wales or cords	sports and casual wear, coats and suits		x	x			
Crepe	any weave	fine, crinkly, moss surface from tightly, twisted yarns	dresses, evening wear and lingerie	x	x	x	x		x
Crepe de Chine	plain weave	light, finely crinkled surface with a lustrous finish	evening wear, lingerie, dresses, and blouses			x	x		
Cretonne	plain, twill, or satin weave	muted, warp-printed fabric with a plain-coloured weft	casual wear		x	x		x	
Crinoline	plain weave	coarse, open weave — sized for stiffness	interlining		x				
Damask	Jacquard weave	firm, lustrous, reversible fabric with a satin ground-weave	late afternoon, evening wear	x	x	x	x	x	x
Denim	twill weave	stout, coarse weave generally with a white weft	sports and casual wear		x				
Dimity	plain weave	fine, sheer, corded fabric	dresses, children's wear and blouses		x				
Doeskin	satin weave	very fine fabric with a smooth but napped surface	sports and casual wear, coats and suits	x	x	x			
Donegal	plain or twill weave	tweed-type fabric with coloured nubs woven in	casual wear, coats and suits	x	x	x			
Drill	twill weave	heavy, firm fabric	sports and casual wear, uniforms		x				
Duck	plain weave	closely woven fabric	sports and casual wear		x				x
Duvetyn	twill weave	soft, velvet-like finish	coats, suits and dresses	x	x	x	x		
Faille	rib weave	soft, firm fabric with horizontal ribs	evening wear, dresses, coats and suits		x	x	x		x
Felt	felted	thick, compacted fibres	millinery and sports wear						x
Flannel	plain or twill weave	lightweight fabric with a soft napping to the surface	dresses, suits and coats	x	x	x			
Flannelette	plain or twill weave	soft fabric, lightly napped on one side	children's wear and lingerie		x				

				W	C	R	S	L	O
Foulard	twill weave	light, soft fabric, usually printed	dresses, blouses and scarves	x	x	x	x̄		x
Gaberdine	twill weave	firm, tight weave with a hard finish	suits, coats, rain wear, sports and casual wear	x	x	x			x
Georgette	plain weave	loosely woven, sheer fabric with a dull, crepe surface	dresses, blouses, lingerie			x	x		
Gingham	plain weave	yarn-dyed checks and stripes	sports wear, dresses and children's wear		x				
Grosgrain	rib weave	hard finish with pronounced ribs	evening wear, ribbons and trimmings		x	x	x		x
Herringbone	herringbone weave	tweed-like fabric made from coarse yarns	coats, suits, sports and casual wear	x	x	x	x	x	x
Homespun	plain weave	coarse, irregular surface	sports and casual wear	x	x	x			
Honeycomb	honeycomb weave	rough-textured fabric with a raised-square or diamond pattern	sports and casual wear	x	x	x			
Hopsacking	basket weave	coarse yarns in open weave	sports and casual wear	x	x	x	x	x	x
Huckaback	huckaback weave	firm, semi-rough, patterned surface	sports and casual wear		x			x	
Jersey	plain knit	elastic knit, will ladder if stitch is broken	all styles, knitted garments	x	x	x	x		x
Lace	machine- or hand-made	any weight, fine or coarse	evening wear, dresses, lingerie and trimmings	x	x	x	x		x
Lamé	Jacquard weave	Jacquard patterns with metallic ground, similar to brocade	evening wear and trimmings			x	x		x
Lawn	plain weave	fine, lightweight sheer with a soft or crisp finish	children's wear, dresses and lingerie		x			x	
Leno	leno weave	lightweight open weave	children's wear and dresses	x	x	x	x		x
Madras	plain weave	fine, soft fabric with yarn-dyed checks colour can be non-fast, hence "bleeding" Madras	sports and casual wear, shirts and blouses		x				

* W = Wool   C = Cotton   R = Rayon   S = Silk   L = Linen   O = Other fibres or blends ·

				W	C	R	S	L	O
Marquisette	leno weave	sheer, open weave	evening wear, dresses and children's wear	x	x	x	x		x
Matelassé	double-woven Jacquard weave	thick fabric with a raised, blistered or pucked surface	coats, suits, dresses and evening wear	x	x	x	x		
Melton	twill or satin	thick, heavily napped fabric	coats and suits	x					
Milanese	warp knit	light to medium weight knit with either a dull or shiny finish	lingerie, dresses and blouses			x	x		x
Moire	rib weave	taffeta-type fabric with a water-mark or moire appearance	evening wear, ribbons and trimmings			x	x		
Moleskin cloth	satin weave	thick, heavy fabric with smooth face and napped back	coats and jackets		x				x
Mull	plain weave	soft, sheer, lustrous fabric	lingerie and children's wear		x	x	x		
Muslin	plain weave	lightweight fabric, either plain or with applied surface interest such as spots	children's wear, dresses and blouses		x				
Net	any lace machine	fine or coarse diamond-shaped mesh	dresses, millinery and trimmings		x	x	x		x
Ninon	plain weave	sheer, smooth fabric—firmer than chiffon	evening wear, scarves and trimmings			x	x		
Nun's veiling	plain weave	sheer, soft fabric woven from finely twisted yarn	dresses, children's and baby wear	x					
Organdy	plain weave	crisp, transparent fabric of tightly twisted yarns	evening and children's wear		x				
Organza	plain weave	crisp, sheer fabric with lustrous finish	evening wear and dresses			x	x		x
Ottoman	rib weave	heavy-ribbed fabric woven with more warp threads than weft ones	coats, suits, trimming and evening wear		x	x	x		
Oxford cloth	basket weave	durable mercerized fabric, light to heavy weight	sports and casual wear		x				
Piqué	Bedford cord or honeycomb weave	fabric with varied, raised surface textures—such as waffle, ribbed, and embroidered piqués	sports, casual wear, dresses and children's wear		x	x	x		x

				W	C	R	S	L	O
Plissé	plain weave	plissé printing giving a permanent crinkled surface	children's wear, lingerie and dresses		x	x			
Pongee	plain weave	fabric woven from uneven, wild-silk yarn	suits and dresses				x		
Poplin	rib weave	light to medium weight with a fine, ribbed surface	sports and casual wear, children's wear and dresses	x	x	x	x		
Ratiné	knitted, plain or twill weave	spongy, bulky fabric with a nubbly surface (Ratiné is also the name of the yarn used.)	coats, suits and dresses	x	x	x	x		
Rep	plain or rib weave	firmly woven fabric with a prominent rib surface	coats and suits	x	x	x	x		
Sailcloth	plain weave	firm, medium to heavy fabric	sports and children's wear		x			x	
Sateen	satin weave	smooth fabric with a lustrous mercerized finish	casual wear, dresses and children's wear		x	x			
Satin	satin weave	smooth, highly lustrous fabric—either light or heavy weight	evening wear, trimmings		x	x	x		x
Seersucker	plain weave	fabric with a permanent woven-in crinkle surface	sports and casual wear dresses and children's wear		x	x			x
Serge	twill weave	fine, firm fabric with pronounced diagonal ribs on the surface	suits, casual wear and dresses	x	x	x	x	x	
Shantung	plain weave	slubbed weft giving irregular surface	dresses, suits, coats and evening wear		x	x	x		
Sharkskin	basket or twill weave	crisp, firm fabric with a sleek pebbly surface	sports and casual wear	x	x	x			
Surah	herringbone or twill weave	soft, firm lightweight fabric (term broadly used to designate any twill silk or rayon fabric)	dresses, blouses and scarves			x	x		
Taffeta	plain weave	crisp handle-finish with a rustle sound to a lustrous fabric	evening wear, linings, trimmings and ribbon			x	x		x
Terry	pile fabric	uncut pile fabric with loops on one or both sides	sports and beach wear		x				

* W = Wool   C = Cotton   R = Rayon   S = Silk   L = Linen   O = Other fibres or blends

Name	Weave	Description	Uses	W	C	R	S	L	O
Ticking	any weave	sturdy, firm fabric—generally striped	sports and casual wear		x		x		
Tricot	warp knit	fine, closely knitted fabric	lingerie, dresses, swim-wear, gloves	x	x	x	x		x
Tulle	Levers net machine	fine, closely hexagonal mesh	evening wear and millinery		x	x	x		x
Tussah (tussore)	plain weave	irregular surface due to wild-silk yarn	suits, coats and dresses				x		
Tweed	plain or twill weaves	rough surface, sturdy fabric, often homespun	suits, coats and sports wear	x	x	x			x
Velour	pile, satin, or twill weave	plush surface	suits and coats	x	x				
Velvet	pile weave	woven-in pile fabric on plain, twill or satin ground (Pile can be left uncut. Panne velvet has a satiny appearance and is often imprinted to become embossed velvet.)	evening wear, suits, coats, dresses and accessories		x	x	x		
Velveteen	velveteen weave	short, closely set pile with a slight sheen	dresses, suits, coats and children's wear		x	x			x
Voile	plain weave	sheer, open weave from highly twisted yarn	dresses, lingerie, children's wear	x	x	x	x		x
Whipcord	twill weave	firm fabric with steep, heavy diagonal rib surface	sports wear and children's wear	x	x	x			

* W = Wool   C = Cotton   R = Rayon   S = Silk   L = Linen   O = Other fibres or blends

SUMMARY

PLAIN WEAVE

alpaca
batiste
calico
cambric
challis
chambray
chiffon
chintz
crepe
crepe de chine
cretonne
dimity

donegal
duck
flannel
flannelette
georgette
gingham
homespun
lawn
madras
mull
muslin
ninon

nun's-veiling
organdy
organza
pongee
sailcloth
seersucker
shantung
taffeta
tweed
voile

TWILL WEAVE

barathea
broadcloth
cavalry twill
crepe
denim
donegal
drill
duvetyn
flannel
flannelette
foulard
gaberdine

melton
serge
sharkskin
surah
ticking

SATIN WEAVE	BASKET WEAVE	JACQUARD WEAVE	PILE WEAVE	RIB WEAVE
crepe	hopsacking	brocade	terry	bengaline
doeskin	Oxford cloth	crepe	velour	broadcloth
moleskin cloth	sharkskin	Damask	velvet	faille
melton		matelassé		grosgrain
sateen		ticking		ottoman
satin				poplin
ticking				rep

FABRIC NAMED

FOR WEAVE	FOR YARN	FOR FINISH
Bedford cord	bouclé	moire
bird's-eye	chenille	plissé
corduroy	lamé	
honeycomb	ratiné	
huckaback		
piqué		
velveteen		

GARMENT DEFINITION

Before designing clothes, it is essential to realize the basic requirements for each type of garment and plan accordingly.

Fashion is divided into two groups, the basic classics and the latest fashion fads.

The elegance of quality fashion moves gradually, with changes about every four or five years. These are the ideal buys for those over thirty who are building up a quality wardrobe to look elegant at all times and for all occasions.

The latest gimmick-type fashion is only for the young and its purpose in being inexpensive is that it is to be worn for the season, then discarded for a newer fashion trend.

QUALITY

Always place quality before quantity when purchasing clothes. Choose the best quality fabric you can afford as not only will it wear and hang better, but it will reward you by looking expensive.

It is always more economical to buy one good-quality garment than two cheap ones which will look shoddy more quickly.

With care, good-quality accessories will last for years. A few good-quality clothes worn with varied accessories can ring in numerous changes.

Try to achieve an elegant wardrobe over the years by buying a quality outfit for each occasion. If it is only possible to purchase one quality garment, then buy a coat which can be worn over less expensive dresses on various occasions.

CLASSICAL GARMENTS

Real fashion does not change all that radically through the years, though there is a quick turnover on trendy items. The greatest asset to a well-planned wardrobe is the perennial classic garment.

The traditional classics are never extreme because they are simple in styling, unexaggerated in cut, superb in fit and workmanship with quality fabrics, which all adds up to garments wearable for many seasons and the basis of a modern, elegant wardrobe.

With adjustments to length and different accessories, many old classics can look as up-to-date and fashionable today as when first worn.

FUN GARMENTS

Mainly for the young, these clothes feature the newest ideas and gimmicks, the fashion look and colours of the season. They supply the necessary stimulation needed to prevent the garment industry becoming dull and uninteresting.

By applying the basic rules, it is still easy to avoid those fashions that are vulgar or in bad taste.

FOUNDATION GARMENTS

For many years, foundation garments were static in both design and colour. With the coming of nylon and other synthetics and the advancements in stretch fabrics with new control constructions and colours other than white and pink, revolutionary changes have taken place. Gone is the old idea of squeezing your figure into heavily laced, solidly boned corsets to flatten everything down to a rigid, shapeless form.

Girdles and brassieres are the foundations of an elegant appearance, giving a firm, smooth silhouette. No matter how wonderful the outer garments, unless the foundations are properly laid, the effect will be just short of disaster. By wearing or not wearing the correct-fitting undergarments, a woman can either enhance or distort the line of an outfit. Nowadays, whether you have heavy hips and thighs, too small a bust, a diaphragm bulge, or any other kind of figure fault, the right foundation garments will correct and improve. Inner shape is the underlying power of control and camouflage.

For a slim teenager, a lightweight bra and (perhaps) suspender belt will do. For the older or heavier person, more control is needed. Mature figures are not necessarily fat or heavy but, with the passing of years, figures change as muscles sag and bodies thicken. Sometimes women wear the same size or style of garment for a lifetime without checking if it still gives

adequate support. The most frequent error in the choice of foundation garments is a girdle that is too tight so that a bulge develops above the waistline, and a brassiere that is too rigid, too padded in the wrong place, or cut too provocatively for good support. Foundations can only control unwanted flesh, not eliminate it.

New fashions demand softly rounded shapes and under them gently controlled foundation garments to produce a smooth outline. Since most styles of foundation garments are lighter than ever, the all-important fit must be more precise if you are to get the right kind of support. Better fit will mean greater comfort. For the best result, devote time to a correct fitting supervised by a qualified consultant. Make your motto: "Try on before you buy."

The main points to look for when buying foundation garments are:

> flat seaming
> reinforced panelling
> neat and easy fastening
> two-way stretch that will give while controlling
> woven-elastic band at waist of girdles that does not wrinkle
> downwards-stretch back panel to ensure comfort and prevent riding up
> bra straps that do not curl under
> cushioned straps that do not cut into the shoulders

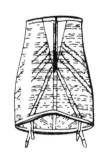

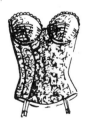

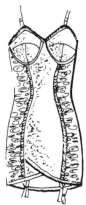

LINGERIE

Well-cut lingerie is a basis of good dressing and, although these garments are not on public view, it is still economic to buy quality. With the use of synthetics, it is now possible to have gossamer-fine lingerie with frills, ribbons, and embroideries which dry quickly when washed and require no ironing.

Hand-made lingerie is still the height of luxury and the styling generally relies on superb cut and simple trimming, frequently with just hand-scalloping at the hem and bodice edge.

Attractive lingerie is priced within everyone's reach and there is no excuse for negligence in the careful choosing of the best style to meet the required need. Rely on cut and quality of fabric rather than garments covered with lace and embroidery.

Foundations and lingerie have always been intimately related to women's outer apparel. These must be co-ordinated with the outer garments, e.g., a low-neck dress must have a low-cut bra and slip underneath. Many expensive clothes have a bra and boning built into them and, in recent years, slips have a built-in bra, eliminating the additional straps which look so ugly through a semi-transparent garment.

Petticoats or slips should always be worn under a dress to prevent the garment clinging to the body and to retain the line of the garment. Slips are frequently built into a garment so that the outer garment falls well. With full skirts, petticoats often have to be stiffened to give the skirt the correct line.

All lingerie should be colour co-ordinated so that the slip, pants, bra, and girdle are the same colour. Where possible, the colour of your underclothes should match your outer garments. The most popular colours are still white, followed by pink, nude-beige, or skin tones which are ideal under sheer garments. Black is the next most popular colour. Bright-coloured and printed lingerie can be fun, but must be co-ordinated to look attractive.

NIGHT WEAR
The choice of night wear is enormous, with a vast array of styles, fabrics, and colours, from tailored pyjamas to the short, frilly bikini types and the long and short nightdresses.

HOUSE COATS
A diaphanous négligé, a house-coat, dressing-gown or brunch-coat can be worn over night wear. Cotton or synthetic fabrics are most practical for summer, and wool or quilting for winter.

DRESSES

Every wardrobe should boast at least one beautifully cut and well-fitted dress. Trimming does not make a dress; cut, finish, and styling in quality fabric do. A day dress is essentially simple, but for an afternoon function a more stylish dress would be better. Cocktail or dinner wear should be high fashion with a décolleté neckline. Elaborate long or short dresses, as rich as good taste allows, are the choice for evening wear.

COCKTAIL WEAR

Dresses with or without a matching coat or a suit styled in silk, brocade satin, or lace fit the occasion admirably. An elegantly styled dress in a plain, dark fabric with a piece of interesting jewellery as the only decoration and accompanied by a hat is the best idea for a wardrobe with only one cocktail dress. The greatest standby for cocktail and dinner parties is the "little black dress" which can be supplemented by other less-stereotyped outfits.

DINNER WEAR

Dinner dresses should be less elaborate than ball gowns, and with a slimmer skirt. The dress should not be strapless but have sleeves or cut-away armholes. It is not advisable to have a high neckline above the collarbone, but a wide or plunge neckline is acceptable.

Formal or official occasions demand long dinner gowns. Satin, brocade, and embroidered fabrics are quite suitable for short evening dresses.

Informal dining on the terrace or patio shows long, simply styled cotton gowns to advantage. Vibrant colours and exotic patterns and prints are not out of place.

THEATRE WEAR

An evening at the theatre is spent, for the most part, in a sitting position. It is therefore wise to wear slim, elegant clothes incorporating an interesting neckline.

Elaborate gowns worn under ordinary coats lose effect. More effective is a plain gown under a dressy coat. The ideal combination is a low-cut dress and matching coat in silk or brocade. Fashion seems to favour short evening gowns except at first nights or on state occasions when the full evening gown predominates. Appearance suffers if you choose a fabric which creases or seats too easily.

EVENING WEAR

Very few women would not want to look their best and loveliest at an evening function. To do this, a woman must use all her skill and feminine wiles. It must not be forgotten that to feel comfortable in a gown automatically helps you wear it properly. The best answer to this problem is to choose the same basic shape as your most flattering day dress, but style it in a rich fabric instead of one more suitable to day wear. Do keep in mind the simplicity of design; rich fabric and non-fussy trimming give the best effect. In some cases, evening gowns are made to look rich through the use of heavily encrusted beading or embroidery.

An embroidered brocade or a lace needs no trimming; it carries its own. Plain chiffon can take frills and pleats. Sculptured draping is decidedly the best method of styling crepe or silk jersey. Organdies, voiles, and cottons are really for the young.

The ball gown may be strapless and therefore may possibly slip unless fitted properly. A strapless bra to the waist will ensure the comfort and fit necessary if the gown has not an inbuilt foundation. Comfort again must be taken into account if an evening gown has thin straps to prevent slipping or cutting.

Well-shaped legs show the short evening gown to advantage, providing that shoes and stockings of fragile appearance are worn. The long evening gown is the more elegant and attractive of the two gowns.

Jewellery to be worn must be *sympathique* with the fabric of the gown. Wear matching jewellery if necklace, bracelets, and earrings are worn at the same time. If the jewellery does not match, it is unlikely to enhance the appearance of the gown.

By the same token, a pochette or evening handbag should be of a colour which matches the gown. Matching shoes and a matching coat will add to the whole ensemble. Should contrasting colours be used, do be sure they are complementary to each other.

Elaborate hairstyles go well with the simply designed dresses, while elaborate gowns call for a simple hairstyle.

COATS

A well-cut coat of quality fabric has two distinct advantages. The first is the warmth it offers, the second the fact that it also conceals figure faults and as a basic garment of a wardrobe should not be overlooked. Frequently the necessity of removing an overcoat does not arise and a striking-looking coat again has two purposes, as an asset in appearance and also as an additional outfit.

Simple styling in good fabric makes the most elegant of coats, where trimming on a cheap fabric has the opposite effect. The classic styles always look better and rarely become dated. To buy quality fabric ensures better and longer wear, and it will fall well whilst being smarter. A coat can be loosely styled, semi-fitted, or fitted, and must hang evenly when worn open. The neckline should be flattering and, in so doing, attractively frame the face. Avoid fancy-shaped sleeves as they only help date the garment. Bracelet-length sleeves are more youthful than long ones.

WINTER COATS

Winter coats are cut generously to allow for the thicker clothing that will be worn beneath. Long sleeves and a high neckline will insulate against the cold. Melton, velour, and tweeds are some of the excellent fabrics available for winter coats.

SUMMER COATS

Summer coats may be worn loose and unlined, without fastenings and a collar, and with sleeves of any length. Linen, heavy piqué, or silk are just a few of the fabrics which are suitable.

EVENING COATS

A coat in the matching fabric of the evening gown is very chic, especially in brocade, silk, lace, or velvet, and far more elegant than a fur coat or stole. Rely on the richness of the fabric to carry the design.

CAPES

A cape must be worn with dash to look attractive. The neck should be fastened, and the position for the openings for the hands must be carefully placed to be functional and comfortable.

RAIN WEAR

Rain wear and accessories have become fashion items, and no woman need look drab when wearing them. As the function of a raincoat is to protect, it should be simply styled, loose enough to wear over other clothes, and be closed from neck to hem with sleeves narrow or fitted at the cuff.

Almost any fabric can now be treated to render it either shower- or waterproof. For general wear, a basic raincoat or cape in a neutral beige or pale grey silk or poplin with a matching hat is ideal because it harmonizes with most outfits.

For city wear, just the addition of a matching umbrella is sufficient to protect you. Oilskins and high rubber boots are sensible for country and sports wear. For the young, there are all the bright-coloured, patterned PVC coats in all styles and shapes.

FURS

NAME	COLOUR	WEARING ABILITY	CHARACTERISTICS
Beaver	warm brown	medium wearing	soft, silky, dense hair
Beaver lamb	warm brown—often dyed many shades	medium wearing	lamb dyed to simulate beaver
Broadtail	usually brown or black	light wearing	delicate pelts with lustrous, moire-patterned uncurled hair from premature or still-born Karakul lambs
Chinchilla	soft grey-blue	light wearing	rarest and costliest of all furs with a fine, silky, but dense hair(Not the most becoming of furs to wear, even if able to afford it.)
Ermine	pure white to brown—can be dyed	light wearing	very silky, short, dense hair
Fox	silver, red, white, or grey—often dyed	light to medium wearing	glossy, long top hair with dense, soft underfur
Kangaroo	red or grey—often dyed white or colours	hard wearing	short, dense hair
Leopard	deep cream to beige or reddish-fawn with black broken rings	hard wearing	silky, flat hair (Quality of coat depends on evenness of markings or rosettes.)
Lynx	deep cream to fawn with black spots	medium wearing	silky, short hair with irregular markings
Marmot	dyed to simulate mink	light to medium wearing	short, coarse, dense hair
Mink	light to dark brown—mutation shades	very hard wearing	soft, glossy with dense hair (Wild mink is thicker, sturdier, and more expensive than ranch mink which is often carefully bred for the mutation shades.)
Mole	brown to dark grey or black	very light wearing	soft, velvet-like fur
Mongolian lamb	brown and black, can be dyed many colours	light wearing	long, soft, curly hair (Used mainly for trimming.)
Monkey fur	brown or black, usually dyed blue-black	light wearing	very long, coarse, glossy hair used for hats and trimming

Musquash	brown-yellow to grey-brown—often dyed to simulate seal	hard wearing	short, soft, silky hair
Nutria	light brown—often dyed grey, brown, or black	medium wearing	short, soft, silky hair
Ocelot	tan-beige with brown or black spots	hard wearing	short, flat hair with irregular markings
Otter	brown—often bleached to be dyed pastel colours	hard wearing	short, silky, flat hair
Persian lamb	usually black, brown, or grey	medium wearing	short-haired with tight, lustrous curls. (The fur is termed broadtail, Persian, or Karakul, according to the age of the Karakul sheep.)
Rabbit	dyed many colours to simulate other furs	light to medium wearing	silky, flat hair (often called lapin or coney)
Racoon	black, silver-grey, or red—dyed many colours	hard wearing	long, coarse hair with dense underfur
Sable	brown—can be dyed	medium wearing	medium long, dense, soft, lustrous hair (Siberian sable is the best grade and one of the most expensive furs.)
Seal	brown or grey	hard wearing	short, coarse, soft hair (Alaskan seal is best.)
Sheepskin	white—can be dyed as required	hard wearing	springy, short, dense hair
Snow leopard	off-white to yellowish brown, dark brown markings	medium wearing	long-haired, with uneven markings
Squirrel	brown or pale grey	medium wearing	dense, short, silky hair

The prestige value of luxury furs has a fascination for many women to the exclusion of practical considerations.

The processing of fur pelts has changed little, but modern tools and machinery have refined the process. To prepare the pelt, the flesh and fat has to be scraped away and the pelt softened and made pliable after a brine treatment. The lustre and beauty of the fur appears after dyeing and other finishings.

In recent years the whole concept of handling prepared pelts has changed. Now fur can be cut, styled, or even draped to conform with the current fashions. Furs can now be worked as other fabrics, horizontally, vertically, or obliquely without losing valuable inches. It is the elasticity of the cured pelts that makes it possible to shape them. The size and shape of the skins is important. The characteristic of mink, for instance, is the "separateness" of each skin.

Quality in fur is just as important as quality in anything. Usually, the better it is, the better it looks. Quite understandably everyone cannot afford the most expensive, but do buy the best you can afford. It repays in wear and appearance. A really good quality fur tie is more elegant than a cheap, full-length coat.

Superb skins like mink appear at their best with simple, classic styling. Where gimmicks and bright colours are required, leave it to coney or synthetic furs. Choice of fur is determined by your way of life—be it for town or country wear. Certain furs such as sable, ermine, and mink are classed as dressy, while others such as leopard, ocelot, and racoon are considered sporty. Frequently, two different furs are used in the making of a coat; black Persian lamb with a black mink collar or a leopard coat with a beaver collar are examples. Some furs, such as beaver and nutria, can be styled to look dressy or casual by the use of buttons or a belt, and be useful for most occasions. Dark furs with a similar-coloured lining of satin or taffeta are the most practical. Furs cut away from the neck are most flattering for evening. Avoid wearing printed fabrics under furs as the marrying of pattern and texture is rarely attractive. Simple classic accessories go best with the luxurious display of fur.

Most women believe that a good fur will never date, but unless it is restyled occasionally, nothing adds years more than an old-fashioned fur coat. Furs, like any other articles of clothing, collect dust and dirt so it is wise to have them cleaned once a year. In addition to removing the dirt, the colour and lustre return, giving a new appearance. Cold storage is advisable during the summer, and a reputable furrier offers these facilities.

SUITS

One of the most useful garments in a well-planned wardrobe is a suit. Selected carefully it can double for any number of occasions, be they formal or informal and the changes come from the clever use of accessories. Gone are the old-fashioned conceptions of a suit — a tailored, masculine style in grey worsted with single buttoning. The variety today is enormous, and a well-chosen suit featuring the general fashion trends will often be more wearable for several seasons than the latest exaggerated styling.

In choosing a suit, take the same care as you would with a coat. Quality fabric with body, such as linen, wool, or heavy silk, and superb cut will always stand out. Necessary care on fit must be taken to ensure correct fit at the shoulders and bustline. The jacket must be moulded to the figure without clinging in an unbecoming way. The collar must fit well, particularly at the back of the neck and the lapels should "roll." The sleeves certainly must not twist or wrinkle when set into the armholes. The buttonholes must be well made — either piped or bound. The lining must be selected with care if the jacket is worn open. An attractive touch is to have the lining matching the blouse which gives an expensive look to the suit. Slim skirts should be fully lined to prevent seating.

Suitable travel and morning wear is a plain-styled suit worn with or without a tailored shirt or a sweater underneath. Medium-heeled shoes, gloves, and a handbag with an uncluttered hat complete the outfit. Jersey and knitted suits do not crush and are extremely comfortable to wear for travelling. Casual wear requires a plain suit to be worn with lower-heeled shoes, a heavier sports bag, coarse, sporty gloves and a bright-coloured sweater and scarf. For lunch and afternoon wear, a more stylish suit with a matching silk blouse and a simple hat of felt or straw will always look well.

Occasions for cocktails, dinner, or the theatre call for the simply cut suit in a rich fabric worn with matching satin shoes and bag. Formal evenings suggest a suit with a floor-length skirt and a low-cut matching blouse or top in heavy silk or satin. The jacket or blouse can be beaded and worn with earrings and a bracelet. If a necklace is worn, then keep the suit plain as a foil for the jewellery.

SKIRTS

Skirts are the universal backstop in any wardrobe and, unless they are made in the same fabric as the over-coat, are never considered smart when worn in town. Skirts are suitable only for casual wear and are generally worn with blouses, shirts, or knitwear.

Straight skirts	Most suits have slim skirts and are elegant only if the hips are slender. For a slim skirt to hold its shape it should be fully lined to prevent seating. If the skirt is below the knees, then a split or kick pleat is necessary to allow for the movement of the legs.
Flared skirts	The most wearable of all skirts which flatters the hips and legs, the flared skirt allows easy movement and avoids bulk at the waist and hips.
Gathered skirts	This style of skirt should be worn only by the very slim and small waisted since gathered or dirndl skirts are often worn with a wide belt or sashed waistband.
Pleated skirts	These graceful, feminine skirts give all the movement of a gathered skirt without bulk or thickness at the waist.
Culotte skirts	These provide ideal casual wear for those whose hips are too broad to wear slacks.
Evening skirts	The long skirt is the most attractive of all skirts for informal evenings. It is generally styled with fullness at the hem and worn with a belt or wide sash.

JACKETS

Long jackets are best when worn with slim skirts, and the fuller the skirts, the shorter the jacket. The bolero, which is shorter than waist length, is becoming when the skirt is flared. It is quite smart when worn over a matching dress. Waistcoats have become fashionable during recent years and, if the jacket of the suit is worn open, the effect is more attractive because it covers the joining of the skirt with the blouse.

Separate jackets should be worn only with slacks and slim skirts for casual or sports wear. They are smarter when colour co-ordinated. Jackets with pockets are best when cut straight or belted.

Fur jackets should be worn only with straight skirts —short or long. Slacks can look attractive worn with a sporty-type fur jacket such as leopard or ocelot.

BLOUSES AND SHIRTS

Once upon a time, as the fairy story goes, a blouse and any old skirt would pass as summer casual wear, with a ring of change to a sweater in winter. Dowdy would possibly describe that outfit today. Blouses now can be made to fasten at the front, back, side, or just pulled over the head like a sweater, and can be tucked in or worn outside hanging loose. There are two types of blouses—one dressy, the other like a man's tailored shirt.

The dressy blouse cut on the bias to give it shape is best worn with a suit. A loose blouse or "shell" as it is known of crepe, silk, or fine wool worn with a skirt or suit of textured fabric is a good combination. A suit with an attractive blouse which matches the lining of the jacket is quite an elegant ensemble. Worn with just a skirt, the dressy blouse can be more elaborately styled with variations of neckline and sleeve treatment in numerous types and weights of fabric.

The trend in casual wear is towards the shirt worn tucked in if the waist and hips are slim, otherwise worn outside. Printed-silk overblouses or shirts are attractive when worn over straight, plain-coloured trousers, colour co-ordinated to match the printed blouse.

A soft, cowl neckline on a blouse or a stark, man-tailored shirt can be worn with a long evening skirt. An embroidered overblouse is elegant when the skirt is slim.

KNITWEAR

Knitwear has at last become fashionable. Knitted, fully-fashioned dresses and suits are excellent for informal and between-seasons wear. Knitted fabrics cut in more fashionable styles are sufficiently dressy to wear on many occasions. A knitted sweater dress is ideal under a casual coat.

Sweaters and cardigans have superseded blouses for warmth and comfort in winter, and have become most useful items in a wardrobe.

Restraint should be used in the choice of knitwear for general wear. Plain knits in cashmere and lambs-wool in solid colours with classic styling never look other than smart. Brightly coloured, beaded, or embroidered garments are rarely in good taste.

There is an endless variety of knits for casual and sports wear. Bulky knits, cable jacquards, and ribs are a few of the patterns that can be knitted in wool, cotton, mohair, or synthetic yarns.

Should you unfortunately be overweight, avoid figure-hugging knitted suits, dresses, or sweaters unless you want to bulge in the wrong places.

ENSEMBLES

An ensemble consists of two or more garments designed to be worn together. It can comprise a dress and coat or jacket, a suit and coat, a coat with a skirt and blouse or sweater.

A dress and jacket ensemble, as well as being elegant, is entirely practical. It bridges the various seasons and is ideal during cooler mornings and evenings. A cover-up jacket worn during the day can conceal a bare dress which can be revealed for evening wear. A dress with matching jacket eliminates the ugly fashion of wearing a cardigan over a summer dress.

Generally, an ensemble is made up of the same fabric and colour or co-ordinated colours, frequently with checks, stripes, or patterned fabric used in combination with a plain fabric. Design features such as square corners on pockets and collars or welt stitching must harmonize in each garment. The different sleeve lengths must be related to each other. The overgarments must not detract from those beneath.

Multipiece ensembles can form the backbone of a small wardrobe and supply garments suitable for all occasions. It is essential when luggage is limited, as it is in air travel.

SEPARATES

Well-planned and colour co-ordinated separates are the most useful in a wardrobe for women on a limited budget, for casual and holiday wear, and for the older woman who wants to avoid the untidy look of odd skirts and tops. Separates can still have elegant couture touches by using excellent cut, fit, and workmanship.

Separates are particularly versatile. Careful planning and self-discipline in buying will be a saving and provide clothes which will interchange with each other. Keep the styling simple and relate the garments to each other where possible. A word of warning—do not expect everything to go together. After all, you would not wear shorts under a topcoat even if they were of the same colour. It is now considered wrong to wear a cardigan over a summer dress or to wear odd blouses and skirts regardless of colour and fabric.

Always build a wardrobe of streamline separates around a colour which enhances your appearance. Choose a basic colour and fabric for your skirts, slacks, and jackets. This will give a "suit" look to the separates. Pick a print or check which includes the main basic colour of the other garments. Casual separates provide the best background for bold, clashing colours.

Where possible, select accessories in one of the colours from the garments, or choose a basic or neutral colour. Keep accessories simple in styling and avoid fussy trimmings.

TROUSERS AND SLACKS

Once trousers and slacks were worn only for casual and sports wear but, with the advent of more tailored trousers and trouser-suits, they can now be worn on any occasion. The colour co-ordinated look of trouser-suits or trousers teamed with matching shirts or sweaters gives an elegant look which is particularly flattering to the larger, older woman. Long jackets, sweaters, and over-blouses are more presentable for general wear.

Trousers and slacks do not look attractive if they are too tight or too short. Long, straight-legged trousers flatter most figures but those with flared legs and with wide, heavy belts or fancy trims should be worn only by those with slim hips and long legs. Jeans in blue denim have become the accepted work wear but, in other colours and with matching jackets, they have entered the fashion field.

Gauchos and knickerbockers, especially if worn with high boots, look attractive on the right figure (slim) but the correct type of fabric must be chosen carefully. A lightweight wool, for instance, will allow them to hang in a soft line, as they should.

Long, flowing hostess pyjamas are very feminine and practical for evenings at home or for patio parties. Fabrics such as lace and brocade tailored into trouser-suits are particularly elegant for evening wear.

RESORT WEAR

Resort or beach wear consists of casual clothes to be worn in the sun. Casual clothes can have high or low necklines either at the front or back, and bare midriffs. They can be tent-like in shape or figure-hugging as a knitted, stretch jumpsuit. They can be shorts, slacks, skirts with tops, or loose casual dresses. Most sun dresses have a built-in bra so that the straps can be detached and allow an even suntan, for it is ugly to see white strap marks whilst wearing a bare-shouldered evening dress.

Fabrics should generally be washable. Exotic, vivid prints and clear, bright colours look best in sunlight, the subtle shades such as moss and ochre look muddy, and pastel colours can appear insipid.

The basic equipment for beach wear is a swimsuit, bathing cap, giant-size beach towel, a large-brimmed hat, sun glasses, a suitable covering for the swimsuit when not on the beach and, for personal articles, a large waterproof bag.

Over swimwear you can wear a loose dress, skirt, or shorts with a matching shirt or top, poncho, tabard, jacket, or a wrap-round shift. This added cover can lead you from the water to the terrace without looking too undressed and offer protection against the burning sun or chilly breeze.

SPORTS WEAR

SPECTATOR SPORTS

Except for the races, which have become more of a social event to parade the latest fashions, most spectator sports require plain, understated clothes. The degree of casualness depends on whether it is a town or country event, indoors or outdoors, and the facilities offered.

If the event is held in a town, a hat is sometimes required, a simple-styled felt or straw depending on the season, while in the country a scarf is frequently adequate for windy occasions. For summer, well-cut linen or cotton trouser-suits, dresses, or knitted suits worn with gloves and handbag. For winter, a topcoat or sporty fur jacket, trouser-suits, tweeds, boots, gloves, and a chunky handbag or shoulder bag.

Watching football or similar games in an open stadium or arena in winter can even find you wearing trousers with a thick sweater under a showerproof duffle-type coat, wool gloves, and a hood or knitted cap, with boots or chunky casual shoes.

ACTIVE SPORTSWEAR

This is one fashion field where you generally have to conform by wearing the correct attire for the sport in which you are participating. The fashion trends are slow to change as the traditional classic styles are correct and always accepted. It is possible to dress for sport and still be elegant by following the basic rules of simplicity, good taste, and grooming.

The particular sport generally dictates the type of clothes, footwear, and gear required. Freedom of movement is essential, and clothes must not restrict in any way, but should be comfortable, practical, serviceable, and appropriate.

GOLF
Choose the classic styling of a slightly gored skirt or one with a deep, inverted pleat worn with a matching shirt or sweater. Light- or medium-tone neutrals or soft, misty colours are ideal. Avoid all white or black ensembles if you wish to appear elegant. Special spike-soled shoes must be worn on the green.

In America, Bermuda-length shorts are allowed by most clubs, but unless the wearer is very young and leggy, they are ugly. Culottes are more flattering and an acceptable substitute.

HIKING
Stout, comfortable, flat-heeled shoes with non-skid surface are the first essential. A skirt with either gores or a box pleat, culottes, slacks, and a shirt or sweater are comfortable. A waterproof jacket with a pleated action back with ample pocket space for stowage will leave the hands completely free. Should the hike be of several days' duration, use a knapsack with non-chafing straps.

ICE SKATING
Skating is one of the most graceful of sports, requiring tights worn under a very short, flared skirt with a waist-length, fitted jacket, a fur bonnet, and white boots. The older woman should wear a longer skirt and a sweater for warmth.

Avoid the fancy-dress look of sequins and satin unless you are taking part in an exhibition.

INDOOR BOWLING

The main requisite for indoor bowling is a special type of shoe to prevent sliding. A sweater or a short-sleeved shirt worn with a gored skirt, culottes, or trousers will allow ample movement.

OUTDOOR BOWLING

Once considered a sport for older women, bowling is becoming popular with the younger generation. Specially soled shoes without heels must be worn to ensure no danger to the turf. Clubs rule on the type of clothes that can be worn.

RIDING

There is correct attire for all equestrian occasions but, unless you are an expert horsewoman, it is better to be more informally dressed.

For general riding, choose beige or tan breeches, a white shirt with a stock, a gold stock-pin, tan or string gloves, black or brown boots, with a black or brown hunting cap. For more casual or informal riding, jodhpurs and shoes worn with a white shirt or a polo-neck sweater is becoming.

HUNTING

The classic attire for hunting is always of superb cut and complete simplicity in each garment. A white hunting shirt is worn with a separate stock and gold stock-pin worn horizontally, a canary yellow waistcoat with plain gold buttons, a black riding coat, buff or tan breeches, black boots, and chamois yellow or white string gloves. The hair should be pinned up in a bun or neatly secured under a black hunting bowler. The famous hunting pink is worn by men only.

SHOOTING

Wear to the shoot a tweed, gaberdine, or corduroy gored skirt, culottes, or trousers, a warm shirt or wool sweater under a waterproof jacket with a pleated action-back and ample stowage pockets, a Tyrolean-type hat, and boots or heavy shoes with thick stockings or tights.

Soft, misty colours that blend into the countryside, such as brown, green, beige, russet, and gold, are the most appropriate to wear.

SKI WEAR

Comfortable ski wear consists of tapered, stretch ski-pants with an underfoot strap or "stirrup" worn over long tights with a fine shirt under a long, bulky sweater.

Over this, wear either a quilted, waterproof parka or a lightweight nylon "shell" with ample-sized armholes for movement, high-closing neck, and protective cuffs. These jackets generally have a front-zipper closure. Gloves, a cap, and ski-boots are essential for warmth.

This practical outfit looks best in one colour of either all-black, navy, or beige. The more eye-catching colours are left to the spectator non-skier.

Knickerbockers and ski-shirts should only be worn by the young, expert skier. Even then, it does not look as attractive as the classic attire.

APRES-SKI WEAR

Wear the more adventurous colours for after-ski wear. Slim-leg pants or flared, felt, or gathered skirts worn with a matching silk shirt, sweater or printed over-blouse and plain, ballerina-type slippers usually fill the bill.

For outdoor wear, seal-hair snowshoes can be worn as they do not absorb the moisture. Wear black shoes or boots with dark clothing, and beige with light-coloured garments. A thick, wool jacket over ski-pants will complete your outfit.

TENNIS

Still the most attractive and suitable attire is the classic white, sleeveless dress with a short, pleated skirt worn with white short socks and white rubber-soled plim-solls. For informal games, white shorts and a white top can be worn. The only disadvantage is that the top frequently separates from the shorts and gives an untidy appearance.

YACHTING

The most advisable clothing is slacks or shorts worn with a cotton top or shirt, bare feet, or flat non-slide espadrilles or plimsolls. Wear a polo-neck sweater and a pea jacket in cooler weather, and oilskins in wet or rough weather. Never wear a dress or skirt on board, nor shoes with heels which will pit and mar the surface of the deck.

76

WATER SPORTS

SWIMMING

With the advent of synthetics and stretch fabrics, swim wear has changed more than any other field of fashion during the past fifty years. From neck-to-knee costumes to brief bikinis, the change has been tremendous. Special bra-construction in a swimsuit eliminates the flat look of the twenties and the thirties to give a natural shape to the figure. Quick-drying synthetic fabrics with built-in stretch ensure figure control.

For the serious swimmer, diver, or surfer, the essential feature of a swimsuit is that it stay in position when worn and that the shoulder straps should not slip or chafe. Two-piece suits and bikinis are mainly worn for less energetic swimming and for sunbathing. They should be worn only by the slim and the young as too much unharnessed flesh oozing out of a swimsuit is very ugly.

Fashion has now been introduced into bathing caps, giving a greater variety of attractive colours and shapes. Wear a plainly styled, one-colour swimsuit with a fancy, multicoloured cap. A more colourful and decorated suit requires a plainer cap.

SKIN DIVING

A rubber wet-suit worn over an ordinary swimsuit is necessary for warmth under the water. A classic-styled suit is the best, as one with trimming will always get squashed. Rubber flippers, weighted belt, face mask and aqualung complete the diving gear.

WATER-SKIING

A waist-length life-jacket is generally worn over a swimsuit when learning to be proficient. For the expert skier, a one-piece or two-piece suit construction that stays in position is essential. A rubber wet-suit gives added protection.

MATERNITY WEAR

Although maternity is far from being the most elegant period of a woman's life, it is now possible to dress smartly with today's fashion. Skilfully designed clothes with good cut and shaping in well-chosen fabrics are the best form of camouflage. It is not essential to have a vast wardrobe for this occasion, a few carefully chosen pieces will do. Select clothes that will co-ordinate with current coats and accessories and colours you look best wearing. Be sensible and wear correct-fitting foundation garments and comfortable shoes. Good grooming is never more essential than at this time.

Choose fabrics that do not show every mark, are easy to maintain, and will stand up to continuous wear for several months without losing their shape.

Camouflage can be accomplished by focusing attention on the upper part of the garment: eye-catching necklines, interesting sleeve treatment, well-placed jewellery or trimming to divert the eye. Avoid obvious waistlines unless high under the bust. Gathers, pleats, and fullness should be kept to a minimum and not draw attention by obviously splaying out over the stomach. Smocks of obviously ample proportions are no longer necessary.

Ideal garments are trapeze, slim-tent, A-line, or Empire-line styles fitted at the shoulder and over the bust to flare out at the hemline. Loose styles are more comfortable and cooler to wear, as they do not constrict the waistline. Choose slim dresses worn with loose, straight jackets and coats, or pinafore-style dresses that can be worn with or without a blouse or sweater or under smart, unfitted coats and with attractive hats. Slim slacks or trousers with expanding waistlines worn under loose, long tops or shirts are suitable for casual wear. Specially designed swim wear with a matching loose jacket is suitable for the beach. For evening wear, choose fabric with body which allows it to stand away from the figure. Avoid jerseys which cling too closely to the figure, silhouetting every curve. Full-length coats or stoles are excellent for a covering.

CHILDREN'S WEAR

Unsuitable clothing for children is decidedly out. At no stage should a child be dressed like a miniature adult, because there is now sufficient variety of clothing to retain a youthful appearance.

Trapeze and A-line styles allow for natural growth without restricting waistlines which rise alarmingly and constrict across the chest within months of buying. It is never too early to co-ordinate separates— blouses, skirts, shorts, and beach wear. Sweaters and skirts worn over coloured, wool tights are practical and warm for winter. Loose styles are suitable for summer. Minimize accessories which will mean fewer but more sensible purchases. Shoes, socks, and gloves have to be renewed frequently because of growth.

Fabrics like sailcloth, cord, twills, and denims supply tough, rough play clothes for girls and boys alike. With the advent of synthetics, grandmothers and children can indulge in sheers and frilly dresses which require no ironing. Children are no longer required to wear pastels (which soil easily). Gay and dark colours are now accepted for any child able to crawl or walk.

ACCESSORIES

Accessories such as handbags, gloves, shoes, and hats are among the most important items for an elegant appearance. It is well worth spending as much as you can afford on accessories for they will give clothes a more expensive look and add prestige to an ensemble.

In a well co-ordinated wardrobe, very few quality accessories are required if colour is kept to a minimum. Naturally, the more colour in your wardrobe, the more accessories required. Keep accessories plain and as tasteful as possible. Too much detail will appear fussy and detract from the ensemble. Accessories should harmonize without stealing the show. Never let accessories overpower a garment; they should enhance it.

Co-ordinate accessories and jewellery with the current fashion to project the complete look. Plan and choose well. Brightly coloured and novelty accessories are never considered elegant and should be used only by the young.

Colour co-ordination is essential to elegance. The most practical choice is black, navy, or brown for general wear with beige or white as additional colours for summer. Beige is much smarter worn with pastels than is white, which can be too stark. Solid colours in accessories can stand repetition, where patterned fabric can be used in one place only. The darkest shade in the pattern is best to use for the basic colour of accessories. Since this is almost invariably black, brown, or navy, these follow the principle that accessories are smarter in basic colours. When you cannot match accessories with every outfit, choose neutral or basic colours.

To make an all-dark or all-light-coloured ensemble less monotonous, relieve it with touches of another colour, with another shade of the same colour, or contrast it with either a hat or gloves. Do not use all accessories in a second colour, thus avoiding a "spotty" appearance. The following guide will assist in selection.

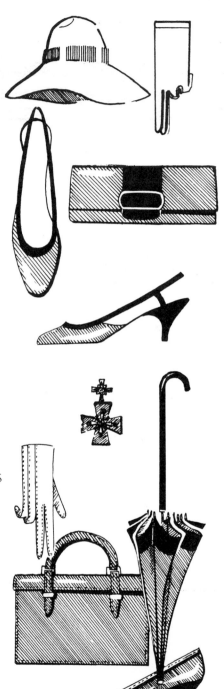

BASIC COLOUR	ACCESSORY COLOUR		ACCESSORY COLOUR WITH CERTAIN SHADES	
Blue	black	navy		
	beige	white	tan	brown
Brown	brown	beige	black	white
Green	black	tan	navy	
	brown	beige		
Red	black	white	brown	navy
	beige			
Yellow	white	beige	navy	
	brown	tan		

Wear dark clothing with a light-coloured hat and gloves, or hat and handbag, or light-coloured hat and gloves. Wear light clothing with a dark-coloured hat or shoes and handbag, or a dark-tone scarf.

LEATHER

Leather has a surface from which all the hair, bristles, or wool has been removed from the outer skin. Suede leather is given a velvet-like nap finish to the inner or flesh surface of the skin. Garment or accessory shape must come from the cut because leather cannot be shrunk or moulded. Skins vary in size and have to be joined skilfully except for accessories or small garments. Skins require specialist care at all times, especially for cleaning, if the surface and wearing ability is not to be impaired.

Alligator Because of the distinct markings of alligator or crocodile skin handbags or shoes, they should only be worn with plain fabrics. Patterned and textured fabrics tend to look messy if mixed with other distinct markings.
Alligator is never considered dressy and should be worn only for sports wear and travelling. It is a very hard wearing skin.

Antelope Antelope is the dressiest of leathers for handbags and shoes. Care must be taken in the use of the skin because it marks very easily.

Calfskin Calfskin is the most elegant of leathers for town wear, and is ideal for handbags, shoes, and belts. It can be styled into most designs.

Cowhide Cowhide is generally casually styled with saddle stitching and brass studs for sporty bags and belts, and is very hard wearing.

Kidskin The most elegant gloves in the world are made from glacé kid, which is often lined for winter wear.

Lizard Lizard skin is dressier than alligator, and used for shoes and handbags to be worn with plain, tailored clothes.

Patent leather Patent leather is only smart in black for shoes, handbags, and belts.

Pigskin Pigskin and peccary is strictly for casual or sports wear, and suitable for accessories and expensive hand luggage.

Suede The best suede is from kidskin, although there are many other types on the market. Suede is dressy for shoes and handbags, but not as elegant as calfskin.

BELTS

A well-made belt can add the finishing touch to an outfit. Belts look best if classic in styling and contour-shaped to fit, regardless of width. If the waist is small, a wide sash or cummerbund can show it off to advantage. Belts in calfskin or matching fabric of the garment are best for general wear. Pigskin and cowhide are suitable for casual sports wear.

Novelties such as chains, studded leather, or ornaments hanging from the clasp should be worn only by the young and the brave. Garment styling should be simple if the belt is fancy.

UMBRELLAS

An umbrella is a fashion item and a necessity in wet weather. It should match other accessories. A really elegant umbrella is plain-coloured, with matching handle and cover. Any novelty in the form of handles, shape, or printed fabric will not only limit its use but add fussiness to the overall picture. Folding umbrellas are never smart, but useful for travelling.

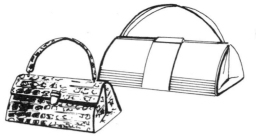

HANDBAGS

A simply styled handbag will not clash with the garments for afternoon or general wear. Make sure that the clasp on the bag is plain and of good quality so that it will not detract from the design of the bag. Quality repays by lasting longer and looking more elegant.

A fine calfskin is the most practical choice of leather and is very hard wearing. Suede is dressier and more fragile, but will mark more easily. Lizard or snake is suitable for wearing with less dressy garments. For travel and casual wear, a larger handbag is more useful. Styling is usually sporty and in hard-wearing skin of calf, pigskin, or alligator. Patent leather is never considered really elegant, although it is occasionally in vogue and fashionable for a season. Black is the only colour which never looks cheap and vulgar. For summer, a beige or bone handbag in either straw or calf is a good choice. White handbags are really only suitable for resort or beach wear.

Today, with such great steps in the plastics field, there are some exceedingly good imitation leathers in elegant shapes on the market. It is better to buy an expensive, vinyl handbag than a cheap leather one that will show signs of wear and look shoddy quickly.

Evening bags should be in silk, velvet, satin, or brocade to match your gown or evening coat. With a chic, black dinner dress, carry a small antelope bag. Beaded bags are only smart in dark, solid colours. Multicoloured bags give a fussy appearance to the outfit and are in bad taste.

GLOVES

Gloves are the most essential accessory a woman can wear, even when not wearing a hat. Like other accessories, they should be chosen with care. Glacé kidskin is the most elegant skin for gloves. Suede and antelope are dressier but easily marked. Gloves heavily stitched in pigskin or chamois are reserved only for sport and casual wear.

Choose classic-style gloves devoid of bows, embroidery, shirring, or cut-out designs unless the garments are plain and clutter-free. Very short or very long gloves are the most suitable with sleeveless or short-sleeved garments. When wearing three-quarter length sleeves, choose gloves long enough to cover the ends of the sleeves. Either medium-length or short gloves can be worn with long sleeves.

Gloves, like shoes and handbags, are more chic in the basic colours of black, brown, navy, bone, and white. Pale beige gloves worn with an all-black ensemble are less obvious than white and are just as dressy. Heavy, dull, opaque nylon gloves which are washable are now accepted as the most practical of white gloves, and must be spotless at all times.

HANDKERCHIEFS

On all occasions, white handkerchiefs of very fine linen or cotton with a hand-rolled edge are the best. Initials can either be embroidered or woven discreetly in a corner in white. Remember to be well groomed; a clean one every day is a necessity. Only the very young should carry coloured handkerchiefs.

SCARVES

These items are ideal in silk and worn tucked into a high, severe neckline. A scarf supplies a splash of colour to an otherwise uninteresting outfit. It is not considered chic to wear a scarf folded into a triangle and worn peasant-style over the head. A hat or a cap is smarter and far more practical.

FOOTWEAR

The most flattering shoes are still plain, classic court shoes with rounded or squarish toes with slim, medium-height heels made of good quality calf, suede, or satin. Always check the fit of shoes and settle for well-made shoes; ill-fitting and inferior shoes make a woman look tired, bad-tempered, and far from elegant. Never wear high heels unless your ankles are slim enough and you can walk gracefully without giving the appearance of teetering or being thrown forward.

Skin shoes of alligator or snakeskin are not really dressy and are better worn for less formal occasions. Medium-stacked heels on leather shoes are suitable for casual wear. Flat-heeled shoes should be worn only with casual sports wear, and with any length of trousers or shorts. Worn with day or afternoon clothes they make the woman look dowdy. Sandals look best with tanned, bare legs, and well-cared-for feet, and with simple summer clothes for seaside and resort wear. Never wear sandals in town unless the toes are covered, as they are too casual.

If you are unable to colour-match shoes with every outfit, choose basic black, navy, brown, or beige. Black can be worn with almost everything except pastels, which make it look heavy and clumsy. Beige shoes the same shade as the stockings give an elongated silhouette if worn with pastels. White shoes should only be worn with white dresses. Avoid heavily styled white shoes as they make the feet look enormous. Leave bright-coloured shoes of red, orange, green, or purple to teenagers.

Use dyed satin shoes to match your evening gown rather than choosing shoes of gold or silver to wear with every colour. Metallic-coloured sandals are best when worn with lamé or beaded gowns.

BOOTS
Boots have been high fashion at various periods over the years. The more elegant boots are styled in the finest leathers and suedes and are designed to be pulled on, not zipped or tied. They should hug the leg like a second skin. Boots can be any length from ankle to mid-thigh. Their styling can include zippers, lace-ties, buckles, or fur trimmings and can vary in colour from the more conservative black and brown to vivid orange or purple. Some boots are made from multicoloured suedes which give a harlequin appearance. Short leather or fur boots are ideal for après-ski or outdoor winter wear, with trousers.

FOOTWEAR FOR SPORTS
Special footwear is required for most sports, usually to grip the surface and prevent slipping. Skates are necessary for ice skating, different types of boots are for skiing, walking or mountain climbing, plimsolls are for tennis or yachting, spiked-soled shoes are for golf, and rubber flippers for skin diving. The list is endless. Suitability and comfort is paramount for all types of footwear.

HOSIERY
In recent years, a great variety of hosiery has been made and women are wearing a different kind of stocking through the day from that worn in the evening. Nylon has taken over the stocking market supplanting the pure silk and rayon ones of pre-war days. The gauge and denier of the yarn determines the strength and sheerness of the stocking. The higher the denier, the heavier and stronger the stocking.

For day and general wear, a neutral beige shade will harmonize with most colours, particularly black and a slightly yellower shade of beige for brown and tan tonings. For evening wear choose paler, sheerer stockings designed so that the heel and toe reinforcements will not show when worn with evening sandals.

Tights have taken over from stockings for general wear because they eliminate the use of girdles and allow for easier movement. They are ideal for wearing with "hot pants". Colourful, ribbed tights, thicker than the ordinary type, are much warmer particularly for winter sports wear.

SHAWLS AND STOLES
Shawls are attractive only with a long, slim gown or a skirt, and must be colour co-ordinated to appear a planned part of the outfit. Stoles are generally much easier to wear. Do not wear a stole unless you are able to drape it elegantly around your shoulders, and move gracefully when wearing one. Nothing ruins the appearance of a garment more than stole ends hanging limply down. Stoles may be made in the same fabric as the garment or contrasting fabric and colour. For evening wear, sheer fabrics of chiffon, organza, or tulle lend a romantic air. Heavier fabrics make it possible to dispense with a separate evening wrap.

JEWELLERY
The use of jewellery is a matter of taste and circumstance. It must be selected with great care and worn with discretion to enhance your appearance and accentuate your clothes. As a general rule, when in doubt regarding a piece of jewellery, don't wear it.

BRILLIANT CUT

MARQUISE OR NAVETTE CUT

EMERALD OR STEP CUT

PEAR SHAPE OR PENDELOQUE

ROSE CUT

One important piece of jewellery, well chosen, with a simple dress can be far more dramatic in effect than too much jewellery and an over-dressed look. All jewellery worn should be matching in metal, setting, and stones regardless of the time of the day.

Real jewellery is the height of luxury. The craftsmanship of design and the quality of the stones is more important to beauty than the size of the stones. Small stones exquisitely set are in better taste than a garish clutter of large stones for a display of wealth.

Costume jewellery must not be confused with real jewellery and should never try to imitate the real thing. Like all jewellery, when chosen with great care, it can add elegance to an outfit. Concentrate on a few good pieces to be worn repeatedly rather than a wide array of gaudy baubles.

During the day, wear no more than two pieces of jewellery and a watch. It is considered bad taste to wear jewellery with sports wear. For evening, you can wear three pieces of jewellery and still be dressed in good taste. Multicoloured junky jewellery is only for informal party or resort wear. All novelties in jewellery are best worn by teenagers.

BRACELETS

Bracelets should be worn only if the hands are well-shaped and groomed and the wrists are slim. If the hands are short and fat, do not emphasize them by a showy display of bracelets. If you wear more than one bracelet, make sure they harmonize. Do not wear too many unless you wish to achieve the "slave girl" look. Chunky gold bracelets are chic provided that no other jewellery is worn.

BROOCHES, CLIPS, AND PINS

These items are most versatile and can be worn at the shoulder, at the neckline, on a collar, at the waist, on a pocket, on a hat, or for evening wear on a bag or in the hair.

EARRINGS

Earrings affect the shape of a woman's face. Simple stud earrings in pearl or gold are suitable for day wear. Pendant, drop, or chandelier earrings should not be worn before 7pm. When wearing elaborate earrings, keep the hairstyle smooth and simple to show the earrings to advantage, wearing the hair swept away from the ears. Care must be taken when choosing earrings if you wear a hat or glasses.

NECKLACES

The most universally worn necklace is a string of pearls, single or multistrand. Pearls can be real, cultured, or fake and either graduated or evenly matched in varied lengths. A string of pearls should be knotted between each pearl. Pay particular attention to the clasp as a beautiful one can be worn at the front giving the illusion of another necklace.

Necklaces should be worn inside the jacket of a suit, dress, or coat with a collar and lapels, and only be visible at the neckline. With a suit, wear either pearls or a lapel clip, but never wear both together. When you wear a multistrand necklace or choker, do not wear earrings as it gives the appearance of fussiness and a thick neck. Coloured necklaces and chokers are best worn with plain-coloured clothes.

RINGS

A marquise-cut stone is the most flattering to short or fat fingers as it appears to slenderize the hands. Well-shaped or slender fingers look attractive wearing rings with emerald-cut or the round multifaceted, brilliant-cut stones. A rather small diamond is shown to best advantage when it is styled with other gems. A small stone can be lost in a heavy setting.

MILLINERY

A well-chosen hat can complement a woman of any age. It can soften and shade the face and give a boost to the morale. Buy a hat because it does something for you and makes you more attractive, enhancing your appearance—not just because it's the latest fashion. A hat should be part of your outfit without dominating it. Individually becoming styles best fill the bill. In crowds, at cocktail parties, the most noticeable part of a woman's attire is her hat.

For true elegance, always wear a hat of simple shape that will never detract from the attire. Shopping for a hat can best be done when wearing the garment it is to be worn with, to enable you to judge the total effect in a full-length mirror. Check if it is in the right proportion for your figure.

Never rely on trimming to make a hat. The shape is the main consideration and any trimming, be it ribbon or flowers, should be worn with plain, fabric garments. With a print dress, wear a plain, one-coloured hat or the effect will be too fussy.

The best colours for millinery are complementary or neutral tones. Contrasting colours have more impact worn with dark, plain garments. White felt can be worn throughout the year.

For summer, choose hats in fine, coarse, shiny, or dull straw or made of silk, grosgrain or piqué fabrics. Wear printed or floral hats with very simple clothes.

For winter, fur hats are the most flattering. They form such a wonderful frame for the face. Velvet, good-quality felt, and wool or jersey knits are most suitable for winter.

Never be deluded by thinking that you look more youthful when hatless; you will in fact lose true elegance.

VEILS

Although not always in fashion, veils are the most flattering of all feminine adornments and are best suited to late afternoon and evening wear.

They should be worn by a woman and not a girl. The young should underline their charm with a fine mist of tulle. The more sophisticated will mysteriously veil her face in a seductive coarse, black veil. Only the elderly should wear a veil before 6pm.

Veils should be of a simple mesh and not dotted with sequins or multicoloured dots. Black, brown, or navy is always the best choice of colour. Brightly coloured veils are rarely attractive and generally in bad taste.

1 Turban   2 Breton   3 Beret   4 Helmet
5 Sailor   6 Pill Box   7 Picture Hat

HAUTE COUTURE

The superb cut, fit, and attention to detail, and the hours of skill in creating a model distinguishes an haute couture gown from a mass-produced one. There can never be a substitute for craftsmanship in design, fabric, cut, and finish. An haute couture collection has a profound effect on the fashion world as presented by the top designers of London, Paris, and Rome. A description of the machinations of a collection follows.

Approximately two months before the sketching and planning of a new collection, a preliminary selection of fabrics is made from those offered by the textile mills. It is from these selected, sample lengths that the approved *toile* is eventually cut. The fabrics submitted by the manufacturer must of necessity influence the new collection and by the same token, they are influenced by what has previously been popular. This ensures a continuity in fashion from season to season. Rarely does a couturier commission a fabric to be made, but instead chooses from the immense range submitted by the textile merchants. Often a new fabric is inspired by an interchange of ideas and put into manufacture.

A single sketch can start off a whole series of ideas, and the selection will take place automatically as the worthless designs are separated from the promising ones. From these will come the nucleus of the future collection which generally incorporates four or five basic lines which are expressed in the dresses, suits, coats, and evening wear.

From the sketched design, the toile is cut in either mull, muslin, or calico. The toile is mounted and pinned on a dummy figure, correcting the line and balance as the garment begins to take shape. The viewing of the toiles often calls for further alterations, elimination, and additional designing. When the toile has been reviewed and approved for a live model, the fabric and trimming is chosen. The fabric is held up, draped, and folded, its texture, weight, and body considered when choosing the right fabric for the design toile. Sometimes a second fabric is chosen for a striking toile and the design is slightly varied to suit the other fabric.

The next step is deciding on which model girl or mannequin the garment will be shown, and the garment will be made to fit that particular girl. Frequently when a satisfactory toile is cut and made in the actual fabric chosen, it does not behave as intended and glaring mistakes are revealed. This means a more suitable fabric or weight has to be found, or the design modified or even scrapped.

The models chosen form the basic theme of the coming collection and further planning of the range. A garment can inspire three or four versions which can then suggest other designs. Garments are pruned from a range because they look old-fashioned, are just not liked, or in order to retain the unity of a collection.

A general rehearsal follows the alterations and, when approved, a particular-shaped hat is chosen to suit the line of the garment and complement it. This is similar to what a toile is to the garment, and is subjected to the same rigid scrutiny.

Once the toiles are transformed into actual garments, they are classified. Generally a chart is drawn up to map out the skeleton minimum of day dresses, suits, coats, and evening wear required for the collection, and allows for last minute inspirations.

Then comes the dress rehearsal to finalize the accessories and to check the proportion and balance of the hat with the garment. Haute couture showings generally follow the same order—suits first, followed by town dresses and the more formal outfits, cocktail dresses, short evening dresses, long evening and ball gowns, with a wedding dress ending the showing. Where possible, light-coloured garments are alternated with dark ones; a garment prejudged as a best seller is alternated with a more spectacular creation. Garments eliminated just before the showing can upset the planned order and affect the balance of the show.

On the day of the showing, the salon is sprayed with the particular perfume fragrance of that fashion house. The traditional gilt seats are arranged and the seating order determined. Each journalist issued with a special pass is allotted a place according to the influence of their magazine or paper. Professional buyers are seated according to the importance of the firm or store they represent. They pay a deposit to safeguard against the possibility of not buying anything from the collection. Favoured clients are also invited, and generally the salon is packed with people with all space utilized, including the stairs, to accommodate the crowd. Excitement runs high and the air is electric before the first model appears. After the applause, the champagne flows and compliments and criticisms of the collection are exchanged.

Immediately after the first showing, the press

demands the garments to be sketched and photo-graphed. They are then followed by the representatives of large stores. The foreign buyers are followed by the international clientele, and then by the tourist who hopes that a visit to Paris will include a glimpse of an haute couture collection.

In a couture house, the designer does not work to the requirements of the individual customer but creates his own design ideas. Designers have several personal assistants, a directrice who liaises between the premiers and assistants in the workrooms, the vendeuses in charge of the showroom and the management. Most large couture houses are now run on strictly business lines with outside financial backing. Well co-ordinated plans and established lines are the secrets of successfully run haute couture houses.

Often the older, well-established houses are re-nowned for exquisite workmanship and superb taste rather than for setting fashion trends.

The *Chambre Syndicale de la Couture Parisienne* regulates the activities of the officially listed French couturiers who must submit to certain regulations of the showing of their collections with at least 60 models, twice a year within a set period. The collec-tions are shown in Paris, London, and Rome in January and July. To design a collection for a showing it must obviously be prepared in the opposite season, for example, next summer's range must be designed, made, and shown during the previous winter, and vice versa. All work must be done in the workroom, with the exception of certain specialized crafts such as embroidery. There is also another syndicate for the accepted accessory firms serving the couture houses, and another for milliners. Both abide by the regulations set down.

Only through the syndicate can a journalist obtain an entrance pass to the collections. Each journalist must sign a special guarantee not to photograph and sketch during the showing of a collection. The syndicate dictates the time of the press release of illustrations and photographs, which are not allowed to appear until one month after the collections are first presented. This allows the manufacturing buyers to copy and market their merchandise before the copyists step in.

Buyers must pay a deposit which is deducted from any purchase they make. Manufacturing purchasers have to sign an agreement not to sell or lend their models to a colleague on the penalty of being barred from the haute couture houses. In recent years, rather than buying actual models, manufacturers have been purchasing from couture houses the toiles or demi-toiles with full information about fabric and trimmings, and even paper patterns to reproduce the design. When the design is mass-produced, it is not sold under the designer's name. Buyers from leading firms select quickly with the minimum of fuss because they know their firm's policy and customers' requirements. These people are always warmly received by the couture houses.

During the showing of a collection, notes may be taken (but never sketches) and frequently a purchaser will buy the bare minimum to cover the deposit, while at the same time memorizing the maximum of details of the other models. This deposit is referred to as a "caution."

It is almost impossible to avoid copying and pirating of designs despite the stringent measures taken. If the new collection is copied and on sale too quickly, it loses its impact and a lot of its commercial value for the couturier.

The decisive influence of a collection can be reckoned during the week following the first showing. The reaction of the buyers, fashion magazines, and press help set the prevailing trends. Every season, by the influence the couturiers have on each other, four or five models will determine the fashion of the following season's collection. Mid-season or the following collection generally introduces more new models developing the best-selling lines from the previous range, and introduces new ideas to be incorporated in the next range. True fashion changes gradually.

Success of a new fashion idea has to be reasonably assured before it is adapted by mass production because the cost of launching is too great unless it will be a winning line. A fashion created in the couture houses is first worn by the smartest women, covered by the glossy magazines, copied and adapted until the fashion expires on the rack of the chain stores to be discounted at sale time. Unfortunately a new idea can be killed when, on launching, it is immediately copied and placed on the market with low-quality merchandise.

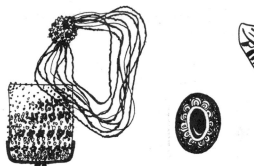  

BOUTIQUES

Originally boutiques formed a part of a couture house supplying jewellery, scarves, accessories, and other special items. Gradually they introduced ready-to-wear clothes and hand-made lingerie which could be altered if required, giving a complete haute couture look.

Boutiques now bridge the gap between the haute couture and mass-produced garments. Better-class stores frequently have a boutique within a department to cater for those who require something different from the general merchandise.

The exclusive boutique shops have mushroomed throughout all large towns and, with speciality shops, supply individual clothes and accessories. Boutiques feature spectator sports wear as well as the dressier and more formal clothes.

During the past few years many new-style boutiques have opened where the prices are relatively low, the décor startling, and the taped music loud. These boutiques are attracting customers from teenagers to the older, more expensively dressed women who are all looking for something different and new to fit the mood of the day.

READY-TO-WEAR

The largest section of the clothing industry is ready-to-wear which supplies up to-date fashion at all levels.

In the early 1850s, ready-made garments began to make their appearance, although it was not until the First World War that they became accepted. After the war, ready-to-wear clothing filled a need for women who were working for the first time in their lives in industry and had no time for elaborate fittings. Fashion was simplified and machinery vastly improved and, as a result of this, women were more sensibly dressed.

High-class ready-to-wear clothing from prestige stores and boutiques are produced in limited numbers, retaining hand stitching and many other couture features. Medium-priced ready-to-wear has little or no hand stitching, and relies on quality fabric and good cut for appearance. Mass-produced ready-to-wear garments have no hand finishing and are found in most shops and chain stores.

MASS PRODUCTION

The invention of the sewing machine revolutionized dressmaking, and complete mechanization of the industry paved the way for ready-to-wear and mass-produced fashions which aim at the maximum number of garments made at a greater speed and lower cost.

A mass-produced garment must have hanger appeal because, if this is lacking, then the potential buyer will not trouble to try on the garment. When a try-on happens, a sale often follows. Colour is the first to attract the customer, then the fabric and styling. An outstanding feature will give the garment the necessary eye appeal.

Designing for mass production is quite different from that for haute couture. After viewing a couture collection, designers for mass production firms often take an original design and copy it exactly or adapt it in such a way that only the basic idea is reflected in the finished garment. Frequently it is cheaper to purchase a toile or a paper pattern of a design than to buy an original model and thereafter adapt it to the current market.

The designer must assess the market for which the designs are required. The price range of that particular market, the labour force available, the number of skilled and unskilled operations, and the weekly capacity of the factory is most important. The right, well-tested fabric at an economical price must be chosen before planning the range. Designing garments for specialized fields such as teen wear, under 5 feet 2 inches or outsize presents a further limitation in styling because size must be taken into consideration.

Before designing a range or collection, a clear idea of the fashion trend must be incorporated to distinguish it from the previous season's collection. The bulk of production lies in wearable garments which buyers consider safe yet of current fashion. A small percentage of the range is of advanced ideas, generally adapted from the latest couture collection; which often forms the vanguard of the next range. These are frequently used for press photographs and window displays and are generally not vast sellers, but more in the nature of a lure or eye-catcher.

Generally a rough list of the type and number of garments intended to be shown is made several weeks before the range is designed, and the various textile mills and merchants contacted so that the designer is able to select a number of fabrics that are of interest. Sample lengths of the selected fabrics are ordered from which the pilot garments are made. Generally, at least two designs are styled in a fabric, ensuring the use of all the fabric. Usually, fashion fabrics cannot be carried through to the following season. Apart from depreciation, old fabric occupies valuable space and runs the risk of spoiling and becoming worthless stock.

The designer must work in close collaboration with the textile mills for the fabric required, with the pattern cutter who interprets the designer's sketches, with the sample room where the first sample is made, then with the production department where ways and means of producing the garment at a reasonable cost to the consumer are worked out.

Mass-produced garments are cut en masse and frequently manufactured on an assembly line where the operators each make a different part of the garment, and only when each section is complete is the garment finally assembled. This method calls for a different way of planning to ensure continuity of production which consequently lowers costs. There are special machines involved which produce various types of stitches, trims, and finishes essential to the final product.

The designer checks the garment through various stages of manufacture to rectify any difficulties as they occur. The design is refined if necessary and, through inspection by the designer and production control staff, it is possible to save more time and costs during manufacture.

A chart showing the progress of garments during sampling is a necessary part of the workroom. A detailed specification sheet listing style number, size range, fabric, trimming and accessories for each garment is essential for an accurate costing.

The final design is discussed at all levels — the directors for approval, the accountant for cost, the sales manager for sales potential and distribution of merchandise. The production manager must state whether or not he can keep production up to sales estimates. The publicity department must deal with catalogues, press releases, editorials, and possibly TV programs. Meetings of this nature keep all departments informed and assist the designer in future styling. Designers not backed by competent management have little or no chance of succeeding in such a competitive field.

BUYERS

Buyers can be divided into two main categories: representatives of stores and speciality shops who sell direct to the consumer, and those who buy for wholesale trade to manufacture and sell to the retailer. Frequently they work together if the model garment chosen is to be manufactured.

Buyers are sent by department stores, shops, and garment manufacturers to view and to buy the latest fashions. Given a certain amount of money to spend and buying at different levels of the trade, buyers must discriminate quickly between a solid fashion-setter or a passing fad, and be prepared to back their judgment with their purchases. A buyer will not necessarily purchase a model to be copied exactly, but adapt it to use as a guide to the line and cut of garments he can sell. Buying in "depth" from a new designer can boost his reputation and assure him of success.

Occasionally a fashion may sweep the European market but not take on in America, while some local fashion may be perennial but never seen outside that country. One example is the American fashion of Bermuda-length shorts, bulky sweaters, long socks, and loafer shoes considered classic fashion wear for college undergrads, but never smart enough to be a fashion anywhere else but on the campus.

Buyers must not only be aware of what is happening in the couture houses, but have comprehensive information about ranges of fabric, all accessories, trimming, jewellery, and millinery. This knowledge is essential as all branches of the fashion world clearly reflect the current fashion story. This wealth of knowledge of the entire fashion industry helps in the final buying.

FASHION REPORTING

Fashion is now readily available to women throughout the world through the comprehensive coverage of the world press and glossy magazines. Fashion coverage is no longer exclusive to haute couture or big name designers, but includes ready-to-wear and mass-produced ranges.

In the fashion centres of the world, the details are reported immediately the collections are shown. They are adapted by city and country people alike. Care must be taken so that you do not slavishly follow the extremes in fashion which are more often shown for spectacular photographs than actual use. Analyse the trends and adapt them to suit your personality, age, figure type, and way of life. Designers for ready-to-wear and mass production adapt the new fashions to suit customers' requirements.

Fashion writers devote space to reports, illustrations, and photographs of those haute couture collections considered good. Adverse criticism of a collection considered ordinary or bad can result in a considerable financial loss to that fashion house. Written reports can be released immediately after the showing of an haute couture collection, although illustrations and photographs are subject to a release date.

There are fashion journalists who write for daily papers whose reports reach a vast public, but their influence is not as lasting nor as great as the exclusive writers' work in the "glossies" or quality magazines which increase the fashion impact with more extensive coverage and colour photographs.

With publicity, the editor of one of these magazines can promote a particular line and colour in conjunction with store promotion or display backed with a vast advertising campaign to ensure that the publication of the magazine and the garments for sale appear simultaneously. This system of collaboration between the press and trade is known as "nation-wide crediting." For maximum impact, all phases must coincide with the publication dates.

GARMENT CONSTRUCTION

FIT

Good dressing cannot be achieved without the proper fit which is important in the construction of a garment. One of the differences between haute couture and ready-to-wear is the superb fit and attention to detail. A mass-produced garment which is the nearest to your size cannot possibly fit you as well as a garment specially cut to fit your figure. A garment to be correctly fitted should move with the body and neither wrinkle nor pull. When buying a garment, check for a perfect fit at the shoulders, and over the bust and hips.

Never skimp fabric and minimize surplus fabric by taking it out during fitting while still allowing for movement. Fabric cut on the correct grain will require only a minimum of shaping and darts. Stripes and checks must match and run straight in the direction intended.

The balance of the shoulder seams is very important to the hang of the garment, which is dictated by the cut of the shoulder line. Check the shoulder line for a perfect fit before altering side seams or darts. Collars must sit smoothly at the back of the neck to cover the seam and to enable the lapels to roll correctly to the first button.

A sleeve should be skinny in appearance yet have sufficient fabric to allow for arm movement. The setting of a sleeve can make or mar a garment and it is not an easy operation to perfect. With a set-in sleeve, the lower the armhole the less freedom of movement there will be. If the sleeve is badly set into an armhole, the bodice and the whole garment will be ruined by dragging and puckering. The armholes on a garment should be correctly fitted to avoid displaying either the bra at the underarm or the straps on the shoulders.

Fit skirts so that movement is possible without showing folds or creases and so that they are loose enough not to cling. When side seams are straight, the garment falls well from the hips and over the tummy and tail. Fully-lined skirts prevent seating or bagging.

Check the fit of a coat or a jacket to be certain that there is sufficient ease across the back and under the arms and that the sleeves are not too tight when worn over other garments. The correct length on a jacket is essential, as it is far more difficult to alter than the skirt of a suit.

BONING

When dresses are strapless or supported by fine, shoestring straps, boning is essential to hold the garment firm and in position. Fine nylon, plastic, or metal bones eliminate the heavy and uncomfortable whaleboning of past years. Frequently a boned bra is built into the lining of a strapless dress to prevent any unsightly lines of a separate bra showing and to retain a smooth outline.

PADDING

Padding can only be used successfully by an experienced dressmaker or tailor. The subtle use of it in a suit or coat can make the difference between a superbly fitted creation and a rough, home-made garment. It is useful to correct minor figure faults of too-sloping shoulders, flat chest, or protruding shoulder blades.

LININGS

One of the secrets of haute couture clothing is the perfect shape achieved by hidden features such as linings and interlinings. This is not an extravagance; it doubles the life of a garment. Quality lining and interlining retains the shape of any well-made and expensive garment. Nowadays all quality clothes are appropriately lined.

Winter coats are frequently lined with real fur, fur fabric, or quilted linings for warmth. Fine wool garments are often lined with organza for body. Sheer fabrics are frequently lined with self-fabric or chiffon. Heavier fabrics are lined with taffeta or pongee silk. It is false economy to use cheap fabrics for this hidden body, particularly if the lining of a jacket or coat is seen. It is very chic for the lining of a coat or jacket to match a dress or blouse.

Linings are generally of woven fabrics which have grain, and particular care must be taken in cutting the lining on the correct grain. If the garment is to be washed, make sure that the lining is pre-shrunk fabric. To line a garment is not always enough because the shaping and moulding of the fabric depends on interlinings and underlinings. Quality linings will always warrant the amount of work put into a tailor-made garment.

FINISH

The more you pay for a garment the more superior will be the finish. Always look closely for this finish in a garment. Do not be afraid to examine the inside of a dress. Points to check: hems to be smooth with no stitches visible on the right side of the fabric, seams over-sewn or bound without puckers caused by incorrect machine tension, waistlines and points of strain to be taped, buttonholes carefully stitched, collars and pocket flaps interlined and pressed flat, zippers inserted invisibly with bulk reduced at the seams, sleeves smoothly set into armholes, facings to be flat and not seen beyond the edge of the garment. The following refinements add a couture touch to a garment.

Expensive clothes should always be appropriately lined. Ready-to-wear clothes manufacturers generally line only the skirt on suits and frequently only partly line the back. Dressmaker-weights improve the line of most skirts and jackets when sewn into the lining at the hemline. Fine chain is a substitute for tiny weights set into hems.

To hold a deep v-neckline in place, stitch one end of a narrow ribbon to the inside point of the neckline and the other to the waistline. Another way is to encase a small weight in a piece of ribbon and stitch it to the inside part of the neckline. Wide, deep, square necklines are held perfectly in place by narrow elastic sewn to the inside of each corner and hooked at the centre back. Off the shoulder necklines stay firm with a short piece of elastic sewn inside the top of the sleeve or armhole. Snap fastener shoulderstrap-holders ensure lingerie straps do not show.

Except when a feature of the garment, openings should be concealed as neatly as possible. Zippers should be as lightweight as possible with the teeth and tape the same colour as the garment and invisibly inserted. A bar tack is sewn at the end of the zipper to strengthen the seams and prevent tearing the fabric. The invisible zipper now makes it possible for the zip to be completely concealed, as the sewing is done from the inside. Hooks and hand-silk bars at the waist and neck hold the placket flat and prevent gaping. When hooks and eyes are used, make a bar of matching thread for the neatest effect.

Buttons must be dyed the exact colour of the garment or be covered with self-fabric. Check that the waist button is in the correct position; otherwise gaping will occur. The other buttons should be spaced from this button.

An inside grosgrain band attached to the waistline of a dress takes the strain off the zipper at the waist and prevents a heavy skirt from dragging down the bodice, and also helps hold the dress in place. Loops fitted to the waistline or underarm to hang a dress on hangers will prevent a wide neckline stretching. It is a wise precaution with knitted garments which, because of their construction, lose shape unless properly hung.

All stitching on hems must be invisible from the right side of the fabric. Thick fabrics require the raw edge of the hem to be bound with narrow ribbon before hand stitching. Circular skirts have a narrow hem to avoid the "pleating" caused by a wide one. The only way to have a wide hem on a circular skirt is to face the hem by cutting the facing the same shape as the skirt. This is often done when a contrast of colour or fabric is required. Sheer fabrics require a hand-rolled hem because a wide hem would appear too heavy. Tulle and net fabrics are just cut off at the required length and left with a raw edge.

Pressing is not only one of the most important finishing touches but must be used throughout the making of a garment. Skilful use of a flat iron and a rounded pressing pad can practically mould the fabric into shape. Hemlines of garments and sleeve, and the edges of collars, lapels, and pocket flaps should remain gently rounded and not pressed flat into a harsh crease.

UNDERLININGS
Underlining fabrics are used as backing for chiffon, sheers, and lace. Firm, lightweight underlinings will add body to the garment and help retain the shape. Cut both fabrics the same shape and handle the two layers as one.

INTERLININGS
Interlinings are generally placed between the garment and lining to retain the shape of collars, lapels, and cuffs, and to add strength to stress points which are pocket openings and buttonholes. There are two types of fabric made for interlinings — woven and non-woven. The former is still the best to use because it has grain essential for the roll of collars and lapels. The non-woven has no grain and can be cut in any direction. Iron-on interlining is attached to the fabric with a warm iron. Interlinings should be compatible with the weight of the outer fabric. The finish can be soft or stiff (depending on the desired effect) to accentuate a shape or to define a line.

PLANNING A BASIC WARDROBE

To acquire a basic wardrobe of elegant and tasteful clothes, careful planning is required. The contents of the wardrobe will naturally depend on the type of life lived. The clothes must be suitable for social and business activities in town and country, or both. Leisure and sporting activities must also be taken into account. In fact, clothes must be suitable for all occasions. When in doubt, dress down rather than up.

If you follow a career, emphasis should be placed on formal suits and dresses with matching jackets — clothes to take you through the day and the evening. During business hours adopt a policy of restraint and moderation. Choose clothes with a definite line, and avoid fussy trimmings and very light colours which show every mark. Select crease-resistant fabrics for a fresh, neat, well-pressed appearance, as a wrinkled look suggests inefficiency. Skirts which are too narrow, too full, or too short should be avoided if you are sitting most of the day. The narrow one will crease across the lap and ride up to expose too much leg. A skirt that is too full gives a bunched look unless carefully spread around you.

Suits that can be worn with or without blouses or sweaters underneath, and two-piece garments with matching jackets will take you through between-seasons weather when a dress is not quite warm enough and a coat is too hot and heavy.

If you are more comfortable in casual clothes, carry the idea over into party and evening clothes. Choose clothes with easy or tailored lines, and let the more sumptuous fabrics determine the degree of formality.

If your preference is for separates, then co-ordinate them with matching colours to give the appearance of an outfit.

With a home to run and small children to care for, you can have a more casual approach to clothes. Co-ordinated separates, casual semi-fitted or smock-style dresses are obviously the most practical and comfortable clothes to wear.

Ensembles are ideal for dressier occasions, while a short evening dress with a matching jacket or coat can double for dinner or theatre wear.

CLOTHES FOR SUMMER

A loosely fitted dress will allow the air to circulate, and a flared skirt will stand away from the legs and not cling. Select a sleeveless, scoop-neck dress in cotton, silk, or lightweight linen as these are much cooler than synthetics (unless of open weave). Short, bare garments are ideal both for the beach and evening wear.

Cotton or silk lingerie is by far the coolest to wear in summer, and, by reducing the number of under garments to a bare minimum, will also assist you to keep cool.

For general wear, low-cut or sling-back shoes are ideal. Wear sandals only for evening, resort and beach wear.

CLOTHES FOR WINTER

Choose a fully lined wool coat or a fur coat with a matching head-hugging fur or felt hat. Wear a coat over a lined dress with a high neckline and long sleeves. For evening, a full-length gown worn with a matching, lined stole will give additional warmth.

A thin silk or wool vest worn under a wool dress will not only keep you warm but look smarter than wearing a cardigan over the dress. Thigh-length girdle or trousers will cover any skin space above stockings. Heavy stretch tights are warmer than sheer stockings, and are ideal for winter wear.

For casual wear, choose thick, wool tights, chunky wool sweaters worn with either a tweed skirt or with trousers or slacks. Over this wear a warm jacket or parka with a hood, cap or scarf for the head, and fur-lined boots and gloves.

Make certain that all outer garments are fully insulated against the cold and wet.

TRAVEL

The era of travelling by ship with vast trunks of clothes has been supplanted by air travel or economy travel where a minimum of luggage is allowed. With the advent of synthetics it is now possible to travel light.

The essentials for travelling are comfortable, practical clothes that do not readily crease or mark. With many changes of temperature experienced in the course of a day, the multipiece outfit is ideal: a dress and matching coat or a suit with a silk blouse plus a matching coat. Always wear stockings, gloves, and a soft hat that will stand up to the rigors of travelling and packing. Fabric or felt for a hat is suitable, but avoid straw as it is too fragile.

For winter, travel clothes can be in wool or wool blends, and for summer in linen, cotton, silk, synthetics, or various fibre blends.

Travelling by car allows more casual dressing. Choose a co-ordinated skirt and blouse or sweater worn with a matching coat or jacket. A gored or slightly flared skirt will prevent lap creases riding up when sitting. Shoes can be low-heeled and accessories casual.

The wardrobe for a sea voyage depends upon the type of ship and the class travelled. First-class travel calls for evening wear. Second- or one-class travel needs only rather dressy clothes in the evening. During the day, sports clothes are worn and slightly more formal apparel worn to lunch. For sightseeing ashore, the most suitable garments are dresses and jackets or casual suits with comfortable shoes for the walking involved. Regardless of class, no one dresses for first or last night out, or when the ship is in port.

For a worldwide wardrobe, consider the list below. Careful selection will pay dividends later. If you co-ordinate colours, styles, and accessories, luggage can be cut to a minimum.

1) Make a list of places you intend visiting.
2) Consider the mode of travel: air, sea, or land —car, train, or coach.
3) Note the time of the year: summer, winter, autumn, or spring, and the temperatures expected.
4) Anticipate activities: sightseeing, business, sports such as skiing, swimming, riding etc.
5) Check accepted methods of dress in each country, such as arms or heads to be covered when visiting certain churches, bikinis not allowed on beaches in certain countries. Avoid wearing slacks and shorts in cities and towns.
6) Make a list of comfortable clothes which are practical and need little care. Items that double for others such as sandals for beach or bathroom, a showerproof coat that acts as a raincoat as well as a general coat, a coat with a zip-out lining or a loose coat you can wear during the day or into the evening.

LUGGAGE

Although you may not buy all your luggage at one time, try to colour co-ordinate it when buying. Brown, blue, green, or black are the most practical colours; white or light colours soil easily.

Select luggage sizes to be useful and easy to manage. It is better to have two medium-size cases than one so large that it cannot be lifted when packed except by the strongest of men. By varying the size, your luggage is useful for a weekend away, a month's holiday, or just an overnight stop.

A lightweight bag which will hold all your toilet articles and overnight clothes and be classed as hand luggage on a plane is far more useful and easier to manage than a separate cosmetic case and an additional bag.

FIGURE FLATTERY

Clothes are very personal and should express the personality, taste, and character of the wearer. An elegant woman is one who discovers her own style and develops it. It is possible for any woman to be elegant if she follows the basic rules of fashion, which are simplicity, good taste, and grooming. None of these need cost money. For true elegance, select simple, uncluttered lines, and colours which flatter. What counts in clothing is ease, wearability, comfort, and understated luxury. Discretion in the choice of accessories, make-up, and hairstyles will also help.

A woman should try to cultivate her own style rather than follow current fashions blindly. She should be able to find the kind of look that can be called her own as nothing builds a woman's confidence more than being appropriately dressed. Adapt current fashions to suit your own individual style and age, avoid exaggeration in dressing, and generally wear basic, classic styles with individual touches. Even in casual wear there should be elegance, with ease and grace the keynote. The time spent in choosing the right fabrics and colours with great attention to fit, finish, and detail, plus care of clothes will add to the image. Style is what you make of fashion, and it has a lasting quality.

It is possible to be elegant without spending much money on clothes if the basic rules of fashion are followed. A woman with few clothes is often smarter than one with money as she cannot afford to shop on impulse and, by planning, buys more carefully and looks after her clothes well. Knowing that her clothes fit and suit her, she wears them with greater distinction. A long-term investment is quality clothes. The secret of being well dressed is making the most of what you buy by spending as much as you can afford on the clothes you wear most, such as coats, suits, and dresses. Save on evening and resort wear because these serve you less.

The first step to being well dressed is knowing what suits you and your figure type. Emphasize your good points and you can be elegant at all times. Choose uncluttered lines, fine workmanship, complementary accessories. Couple with impeccable grooming. Try to find clothes and colours that do something for you, clothes you feel and look smarter in. Colours which make you appear alive and glowing are the most suitable, not dreary, washed-out colours.

If you have an average figure, finding ready-to-wear clothes to fit you is easy, but it does not necessarily follow that you will look good in everything, so choose styles carefully. Wear for all you are worth the clothes which suit you as they do a great deal for you. Copy the shape in different fabrics, and try other flattering colours. This way will give you sufficient variety as opposed to a more extensive wardrobe of less flattering styles. Concentrate on simple, classic styles with good lines and these will be smart and practical in two or three years' time.

If a garment is elaborately cut, use little or no trim. Never attempt to cover poor cutting or designing with elaborate trim. It does not avert the eye from the garment's basic faults. An inexpensive dress need not be cheap-looking. Chosen carefully and worn with imaginative accessories, quality buttons, a beautiful belt or one striking piece of jewellery, the garment can be just as effective as an expensive one. Detail and fabric is what gives an outfit a casual or formal look. Self-fabric trim is smarter than contrast—either in colour or fabric.

Great care should be taken when buying foundation garments, which should be personally fitted. Discard immediately any garment that no longer controls or gives the required support. Ready-to-wear clothes should be tried on over the correct foundation garments. An attractive-looking dress on a display stand need not necessarily look the same on you, particularly without the correct foundations beneath.

If possible, wear the rest of the outfit when you shop for a hat to go with a coat, suit, or dress. Check all views, particularly rear views in the mirror. Only buy clothes which really fit. Never try to squeeze into a size smaller than you really need, then wonder why it looked better on a model. Tight clothes make any figure look plump.

Do not adopt a whole new look unless you know it really does something for you. The effect should be how attractive you look, rather than what smart clothes you are wearing. Follow fashion trends accepted by the Elegants and not just exhibitionists. Avoid extremes in fashion unless you have the flair to wear them. Avoid vulgarity in fashion at all times. Sophistication in dressing is not just putting on too much make-up, too many accessories or gimmicks which come and go quickly—these are better left to the very young.

Regardless of their shape or size, the elegant women who are considered the best dressed generally wear the simplest clothes. They look for flattering, well-cut garments devoid of surplus detail, quality fabrics which will always hang and wear better, smooth fit, and excellent finish bearing the stamp of individual fittings and flattering colours. At no time overdress and, if in doubt, do not wear it. No elegant woman wants to follow fashion slavishly. It is the personal touches which give a lift to your wardrobe. A few really good clothes are all a woman needs if she understands how to use accessories. Women should respect their type and adapt the fashions to suit themselves. A carefully selected scarf, a well-placed bow or clip, or perhaps the angle at which a hat is worn are such touches. A striking effect will be achieved by wearing a contrasting colour or one piece of jewellery. One accent will add interest, but more could ruin the effect.

Your figure problems can be disguised by using clever tricks designed to create the illusion of perfection by camouflaging the trouble spots with careful styling, and superb cut and fit. The best way to accentuate your good points is to emphasize them and reveal them, fit them closely or accentuate them with eye-catching features such as well-placed jewellery or trim.

With a lovely face, wear face-framing hats and striking earrings. Reveal a perfect neck with low and wide necklines, sparkling necklaces, and chokers. If your shoulders are your best feature, display them by wearing off-the-shoulder necklines, bare sun dresses and strapless evening gowns.

A well-shaped bustline can be closely fitted with unadorned bodices and sweaters in figure-hugging fabrics like knits and jerseys. Highlight your perfect curves by wearing satins and lamés. Draw attention to a tiny waist by wearing clothes with fitted waistlines, accentuated with wide belts and sashes in contrasting colours. If your hips are slender closely fit them with sheath silhouettes. Depending on the kind of pleats you pick, you can add or subtract inches from your hip measurement.

Wear shortish skirts with lighter-toned stockings and pretty shoes to show off good legs and ankles. Choose skirts with deep splits and dresses with uneven hemlines to reveal these lovely legs. Where it is suggested that you wear your skirts shorter or longer, it means just $\frac{1}{2}$ inch or 1 inch variation from the current fashion length; wear whichever is the more flattering. Do not suddenly wear skirts almost down to the ankle or mid-thigh when the fashion is to the knees. If suggested that stockings be worn a lighter or darker colour, try

just one shade either way, not almost white or black. Always use discretion in dressing, and avoid the extremes in fashion.

If you have well-shaped hands, call attention to them with cuffs on sleeves, bracelets, dress rings, or coloured nail polish. If their shape is unattractive, leave them ringless and use colourless or pale pink nail polish and, where possible, wear gloves.

Never accentuate a good point if it brings out a bad one. A classic example is a full-busted woman who fits her comparatively slender hips too tightly. This accentuates her lack of proportion and makes her appear top-heavy.

Never leave a bad point undisguised. Mask it, cut it up, or draw attention away by accentuating something else. Stategically placed detail and trimming can divert the eye from a bad point. It must never give the appearance of being added as an afterthought. Before diverting attention from anything, you must first mask it with some misleading line. A thin, flat-chested woman shuns fitted sweaters, but creates the illusion of fullness by wearing a softly draped bodice which accentuates a tiny waist and by wearing wide belts and sashes. She also keeps her necklines high, thus avoiding revealing bones. A large-hipped woman will gently pad her shoulders, wear interesting necklines with wide collars and sleeves that are either gathered at the head or are short with cuffs to give width to the top of her body and offset the width of the hips. A thick-waisted woman will distract attention from the waist by flaring her skirt and focusing attention on her neckline and hat.

Never repeat a bad line. If your hips are too large, do not wear a jacket that ends at this point, nor wear horizontal stripes over this part of the anatomy. Avoid the length of the sleeve being the same length as the jacket as this accentuates the widening effect at the hip line. If tall do not wear a slim-skirted dress with vertical stripes or braid from neck to hem.

Choose fabric carefully. Fabrics that have bulk (such as heavy tweeds or long, pile coatings) will give the appearance of weight to any figure. Plaid and checks accentuate both height and width. Stripes, pleats, tucks, buttons, and seams emphasize the direction in which they travel. Big, bold prints make you look larger. Small all-over misty prints are reducing. Use check or patterned fabrics to highlight your good points and darker, plain fabrics to play down the bad. The shiny surfaces of satin, lamés, and sequins are not slimming; they highlight every curve you have and should be worn only on slim figures. If you are slender, wear transparent and clinging fabrics or jersey as these reveal the figure underneath.

Choose colours to flatter yourself. Remember light colours make you look larger. If your hips are too large, wear a dark skirt with a light-coloured blouse to optically rearrange the proportions.

Suit your accessories to your size. A small woman should keep all her accessories in proportion to her size because a large handbag will look like a briefcase. A large woman carrying a small handbag will look as if she is holding a child's bag. A tiny woman should wear fine, delicately set jewellery. Chunky jewellery is best for the larger woman.

Watch proportions. Keep a sharp eye on the balance of the overall proportion, including the hat. Check skirts, jackets, and sleeves for the correct length.

Consider the outfit as a whole. Critically use the mirror and consider front, profile, and rear views, especially when wearing slacks, shorts, or slim skirts. Check posture for dowager's humps at the back of the neck, sway-back at the waist, tummy or hip spread, then dress accordingly.

Real chic is understated elegance, and flair is all in the way clothes are worn. It is not so much what you wear but how you wear it. The time and care spent in careful dressing will repay you with a more attractive appearance.

AGE

A woman can be elegant throughout her life. The great secret is to adapt the present fashions to suit her age group, figure type, way of life, and personality. As one ages, the skin texture changes, the hair colour fades, and the figure slackens and frequently thickens.

Colours, fabrics, and styles which suited you in the teens will not necessarily flatter you in the fifties, while a lighter or darker colour, a clearer or more muted shade may be more attractive to wear. Classic styling and quality cannot be surpassed for lasting elegance.

IN THE TEENS

If you are in your teens this is the time to wear the latest gimmicky fashions, off-beat and unusual colour combinations. Where possible, tie your clothes down to one or two basic accessory colours, which makes good fashion sense and leaves more money for the rest of your wardrobe.

AT TWENTY-FIVE

This is the time to begin buying quality in a well-cut coat, an elegant suit, and simple, well-cut dresses.

Buy fewer, better-quality accessories which will wear longer and look better than cheap ones.

AT THIRTY-FIVE

This is the age where poise and personality are an asset.

Start spending a fortune on foundation garments. Nothing does more for you and your clothes than the correct-fitting foundations. Do not leave this essential until you lose your figure and then expect miracles from your bra and girdle. Correct support coupled with good posture will carry you through the next forty years.

Avoid harsh colours and pick subtle shades. Choose discreet, yet up-to-date styling for co-ordinates. Take care with casual dressing so that you do not look sloppy or untidy. Overhaul your cosmetics and make more of yourself. Pamper your hands and do not let them give away your age. Pay extra care to your feet with correctly fitted and well-made shoes. You cannot look vital and attractive if your feet hurt.

FORTY-FIVE AND OVER

There is sufficient versatility now in fashion for a woman to select from the younger fashions and make the most of them by wearing what she likes and what suits her best. To look truly elegant, choose clothes which have a soft line and avoid the harsh, ultra-sophisticated or masculine styling and over-fussy clothes and trims. Outfits in one colour are ideal for most occasions.

Select clothes which are comfortable to wear and make dressing easier. Choose front buttoning, extra-long zippers, and garments which can be stepped into or wrapped round the figure. Wear dresses which gently mould the figure, subtly skim the hips. The most flattering skirts are gored, flared, slim, or flat-pleated ones. Avoid bulk at all costs if you want a trim appearance.

For summer, cover the upper part of the arms with short sleeves They are more flattering than a sleeveless garment which requires a firm upper arm. Use a décolleté neckline for evening wear instead of a strapless garment.

Some colours and shades are not particularly flattering to faded or grey hair. Check these in the colour section. To soften the effect of unrelieved black or dark brown against the face, wear pearls or a flattering, coloured scarf at the neckline.

Buy quality accessories which, although expensive, will last for years. At this age always wear a hat and gloves. A too casual appearance can be taken as a couldn't-care-less attitude. Hats with soft brims and veils flatter the face. Immaculate gloves cover the ravages of time on the hands. Wear sensible shoes which can be stylish but still comfortable.

Most women can take years off their age with a smart, well-cut hairstyle. Wear the hair shortish or swept softly off the face. Brighten fading hair with same-colour rinses.

Choose muted make-up and wear soft-coloured rosy or coral lipsticks rather than dark reds, which make the lips look thin and hard.

Remember that the way you wear your clothes matters. You should look gay in them and carry them off with conviction. Zest is the joy of living which shines through and make you more attractive in your well-chosen clothes.

COSMETICS

Cosmetics should always be used with great discretion to give a natural look and youthful glow. The days of the highly painted look have gone; make-up should never be exaggerated. False eyelashes and heavy eye make-up should be used only in the evening. When in doubt regarding the best use of cosmetics, take the advice of a consultant in any large store.

With the advancements in the cosmetic field, blemishes can be covered with the sweep of a skilful brush which still gives a translucent look. Faces can be reshaped by the use of special contour shadow and highlighter cosmetics.

Cosmetics for the older woman should give a muted "soft-focus" matt appearance worn with a light-coloured lipstick, which is younger. Care of the skin with the use of cosmetics will be repaid by a youthful appearance.

PERFUME

Always wear perfume to make you feel feminine and well-dressed. This leads to making you feel and look more beautiful. The allure is always intriguing.

If you are very young, choose a light, flowery skin cologne or toilet water as the full perfume fragrances are more suitable for the older woman. When choosing a perfume, try a fresh fragrance which is not flowery, but sophisticated without being heavy. Use personal research to select the right perfume to suit your personality. Always use perfume sparingly. Nothing is more overpowering than heavyhanded

application of perfume. Wear matching skin cologne or toilet water.

Choose all cosmetics including bath soap and talcum powder to be of the same fragrance to blend in with your perfume; otherwise the result could be most unpleasant.

HAIR

One basic rule for elegance is to discover your best style and never radically change it. Spend money on good style-cutting, which is essential if you want your hair to fall well in all weather and appear groomed under all circumstances. Adopt a coiffure that is simple and easy to manage. Remember that complicated hairstyles, like fussy clothes, are very ageing.

While in your teens, you can wear your hair long, straight, or curly with fringes, bangs, pigtails, ponytails with bows, ribbons, combs, clips, or headbands.

After the age of 30, avoid long, shoulder-length tresses. Choose between a short, plain style or pin up long hair in either a soft French roll or a chignon. Keep the style soft; remember the hair should be a flattering frame for the face. Only perfect bone structures can take a harsh ultra-short hairstyle or hair dragged back from the face.

When wearing hats, the hairstyle must be simple or it will detract from the hat and ruin the effect.

Wigs or hair-pieces such as fringes, falls, and bandolas have now been accepted as an essential part of emergency hair grooming after having spent a windswept day in the outdoors. They transform you within minutes into a well-groomed woman. Buy the best quality hair-piece you can afford. Not only will it last longer, it will be better blended to match your own hair. Wigs or hair-pieces can be elegant only when skilfully used so as to be undetected in a hairstyle.

POSTURE

A woman should try to retain or at least acquire a slender figure—not only for her health but for her morale. When you are slim, you will find you will feel better and have much more energy. This will give the illusion of youth.

What is more important than mere measurements is the way you move. Just by standing up straight you will look more attractive in your clothes. Nothing is more ageing than a slump. By shuffling along with chin on the chest, you will look ninety, and even the effect of a Paris gown will be lost with bad posture.

Deep, low armchairs are deadly for sitting in and rising from gracefully. Do not flop into a chair and then lever yourself out as both give the effect of your being twenty years older and a stone heavier. Walk lightly, but with dignity and "think tall" to be more attractive.

Graceful movement is always attractive. A gliding walk is something anyone can learn. Try walking with the head up, eyes looking ahead, shoulders back, tummy and tail tucked. in, arms lightly at the sides, swinging naturally. With a little practice in your home, you will develop a graceful rhythm. Then try sitting on a straight-back chair for better posture. Sit with the tail well back with knees together and the legs turned to one side with the ankles crossed.

GROOMING

The secret of true elegance is good grooming, for without it no woman can be considered well dressed. The following points should be checked.

Hats	Well brushed, particularly the inside of the headband
Hair	Well cut, frequently washed, shiny, well brushed, and tidily arranged
Make-up	Discreet, carefully blended cosmetics which are almost undetected
Hands	Clean, well manicured, with immaculate nail polish
Lingerie	A slip that does not hang beneath a skirt, shoulder straps that do not show through sheer bodices or open and wide necklines
Apparel	Good clothes must be hung up correctly after wearing, brushed, pressed, and aired to retain their shape and to extend the life of the garment. Check that they are spot-free, without threads hanging or buttons missing, and that the hemline is even.
Gloves	Spotless at all times
Stockings or tights	Smooth at the ankles and if with seams, these must be straight. No ladders visible
Shoes	Clean, well repaired, and in good condition
Body	After bathing or showering, do not neglect the daily use of deodorants and a splash of skin cologne. Clean teeth are necessary
Final touch	A spray of perfume to match your skin cologne

COLOUR FLATTERY

Colour is stimulating and does so much for a woman by enhancing her appearance. It injects life into clothes which will give her more confidence so that she is more attractive. Colour first attracts a potential buyer; most women have a preconceived idea of buying a particular coloured garment. Most stores now display their garments not only in size ranges but in colour grouping. This saves time and stops the merchandise being soiled as a result of over-handling.

Hard and fast rules cannot be laid down for colour as so much depends on individual taste. Colour co-ordination is achieved when an outfit is wholly pleasing from head to toe without being drab or lacking in interest. Use discretion in the selection of colours. No matter how well designed the garments are, or how suitably matched the accessories are, if the colour does not flatter you, the effect of good designing is wasted. Always choose colours by daylight and if they are to be worn in the evening, see them under similar lighting. Electric light can change colours, blues and greens especially.

Colour can be divided into groups as follows.

Soft pastels	Apple green, soft yellow, baby blue, and pink
Neutral and basics	Black, brown, navy, beige, grey, and white
Medium colours	Pink, cool blue, green
Dark colours	Royal blue, burgundy, and pine green
Vibrants	Hot pink, sharp yellow, red, orange, emerald, lime green, and electric blue

Bright, clear colours look best in sunlight; the more subtle colours of olive and ochre look muddy. Apart from prints, avoid using more than two colours in any outfit, and two touches of any one colour is enough or it will lose its impact. The colour exception is sports wear where multicoloured styles are often fashionable.

Always choose a soft rather than harsh colour because it is easier to wear and more flattering. Try tone-on-tone effects. Tones and shades can be mixed and mingled—such as a very pale and brilliant shade of the same colour used together, plain colours used with a dash of something sharp to make them less conventional and more interesting, and vivid contrasts combined with very soft shades.

Create your own colour story without restricting yourself to just two or three basic colours. Choose colours which flatter and enhance you, not colours you have to work hard to wear to look alive. Only through experience will you become selective about colours and tones which compliment or do nothing for you. Check the colour of the fabric against your face. Hair, eyes, and skin colouring must be taken into account, plus the occasion for day or evening wear. Generally, the smaller and thinner the person, the lighter the colour she should wear, with the reverse for taller, heavier types.

Before launching into an entirely new colour or shape, be sure that it not only flatters you but co-ordinates with your current wardrobe and accessories. Never wear a whole outfit of colours you dislike because they are in fashion. Compromise by using them in a print, trim, or accessories. There are shades which are becoming to you within the range of any colour, and it is just a matter of selecting the right tone and shade. If a colour suits you, stick to it, even if you have a wardrobe full of this most flattering colour.

If uncertain about a colour, gradually learn to wear it by commencing with one basic or neutral colour with matching shoes and handbag and use either contrast or complimentary colours in gloves and hat. If colour confident, try the bold groupings, such as pink and olive, orange and red. These are "clash" colours and need careful colour balance to look great, but should only be worn by the brave who do not mind being conspicuous.

Grey and fawn are safe basic camouflage colours which in themselves do "nothing" for you. The skilful adding of a strong accessory colour will make them come alive. Avoid at all times unrelieved neutral and safe, uninteresting colours without this dash of colour. Black, navy, brown, and various shades of beige are good basic colours with which to start your wardrobe, particularly if the size has to be restricted.

Be colour conscious right down to your toes. It will pay dividends. Accessories have taken to colour. Care must be taken with the basic colour of the garments if unusual coloured accessories are to be worn to advantage. Leave the wearing of wild colours such as purple or orange to the young.

PERSONAL COLOURING
HONEY BLONDE
  hair: honey or gold
  eyes: blue, green, or hazel
  skin: pale or peachy

Clear, warm colours and rich pastels add richness and softness to your looks. Colours that are too pale look lifeless against your delicate colouring while harsh, raw colours deaden skin tones.

LIGHT OR PALE BLONDE
  hair: light blonde
  eyes: blue, grey, or green
  skin: fair or rosy

As a light blonde, you must guard against looking too pale and colourless. Avoid wearing vivid, hard colours which drain the life from your already pale colouring. Warm, medium colours will give a flattering, warm glow.

STRAWBERRY BLONDE
  hair: golden blonde with a rich, red glow
  eyes: blue or green
  skin: pale or high colouring

With your colouring, strong colours such as blue, green, and gold are the most flattering as they add richness to your colouring. Avoid watery colours that make you look insipid or brassy colours that contrast too violently with your hair.

LIGHT AND MID-BROWNETTE
  hair: light to medium brown
  eyes: hazel, grey, blue, or green
  skin: pale or pink tones

With hair, eyes, and complexion all a medium tone, you must play up to your gentle image and not over-power it with vivid contrasts, harsh and drab colours. In-between medium tones are best as warm colours and lively shades put a glow to pale complexions and make hair colouring appear deeper and richer.

BRUNETTE OR DARK BRUNETTE
  hair: dark brown to black
  eyes: dark brown, hazel, grey, or blue
  skin: creamy, olive, or rosy

A brunette can wear more variety of colours and shades than any other type. Wear warm, stimulating colours to emphasize your dramatic colouring. Coral, turquoises, and raspberry colours are ideal, but make sure that they are soft in tone because harsh vibrant colours make you look hard. The light, more delicate shades such as aqua or pink heighten your colouring if the skin is creamy or you have a tan. Brunettes frequently have a sallow complexion and should avoid muddy colours such as grape, olive, and mustard as these make the skin and eyes look dull and less vivid. Avoid colours which cast a yellow "jaundice" glow as these are the least flattering of colours for a brunette.

REDHEAD
    hair: bright red or titian
    eyes: blue, hazel, green, or grey
    skin: pale or pink tones

With such striking colouring, wear colours that bring out the richness of your hair colour and act as a foil. Avoid harsh, raw colours that kill the natural colouring and harden the looks. Most blues, greens, dark and burnt colours are excellent to wear. Reds

and pinks can be worn if carefully checked against the face in daylight to ensure the selection of the most flattering colours.

SILVER GREY
    hair: salt and pepper colours to white

Vital, warm colours do wonderful things for your colouring. Warm pastels, soft turquoise and rose colours give an extra richness, while muddy shades such as olive and maroon give a dull lifeless look which will neutralize your colouring.

SOFT WHITE
    hair: silver to white

Rich, soft shades give warmth and do not make a harsh contrast against the hair and skin. Very bright colours will overpower you and make you appear washed out.

FIGURE TYPES

The ambition of every woman interested in clothes is to show herself to her best advantage. Before you do this, you must recognize your figure type. If it is any consolation, very few women possess ideal proportions, and most figures have at least one main figure fault. By selecting the right clothes for your figure type, the illusion of perfect proportions can be achieved. The latest fashions should be adapted to suit your figure.

Unless you ruthlessly face up to your figure faults, you will never be able to disguise them. Use clothes to flatter your figure problems; choose garments which are designed to either conceal or create curves.

Today's beauty standards require the bust and hips to be the same measurements and the waist 10 inches smaller. This is the ideal, but it is rare. Most women have hips 2-4 inches larger than the bust measurement and a waist 8 inches smaller, so that the average woman with 34-inch bust is likely to have 36-38 inch hips with a 26-inch waist measurement.

There are four basic figure variations to the average figure. These are short, tall, angular, and heavy. Decide to which group you belong, first by weighing yourself and then by checking your height. Check your bone structure. It can be light, medium, or heavy. With your height in mind, decide if you are average, short, or tall.

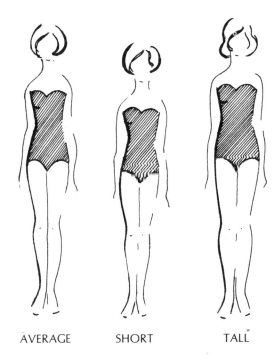

AVERAGE   SHORT   TALL

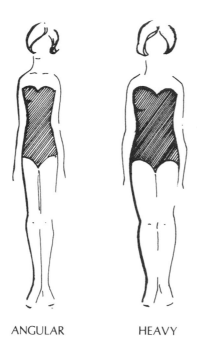

ANGULAR   HEAVY

Run a tape measure around your bust, waist, and hips. This should convince you of your true size where the eye might deceive. With these figures in mind, stand in front of a full-length mirror and take a long, dispassionate look at yourself. Self-deception is no solution to your problems.

If you are under 5 feet 3 inches, then you are considered short and in the majority. You are probably short-waisted and short-necked with short arms and legs which need the illusion of length. If you are under 5 feet 2 inches and well proportioned with a definite, small bone frame, then you are classed as tiny and need only to dress in good taste to look perfect because you have no great figure faults.

You are in the minority as a tall girl if you are over 5 feet 8 inches. You are generally fairly slim with a long neck, long limbs, and a small bust. You will find it easy to subtract inches by careful dressing.

If you are 7lb above the average weight for your height and bone structure, you are starting to get plump. Overweight by 14 lb or more, you are classed as heavy or, if you like, pleasantly plump.

The plump figure needs to pare off pounds by diminishing inches. This figure type tends to be too curvy. The heavy figure is often either hip-heavy or top-heavy which means that the figure proportions have to be visually rebalanced as well as made slender.

If you are 7 lb under weight, you will be slender, and the most envied of figure types because you can wear almost any fashion well. If you are bony and appear gaunt, it is very easy to add on inches to create the illusion of curves and femininity.

If you are of average height and the correct weight, you will have little to worry about and no trouble finding wearable clothes. Remember that every woman does not look good in every style and clothes which look wonderful on a tall, thin girl will not flatter a short, plump figure.

If you are a short, angular girl or a tall, overweight one, there are endless combinations to these basic figure types. If so, choose from the sections which apply to both characteristics.

When you have identified your figure type and its faults, restore the balance by applying the principles of optical illusion by means of line, colour, and emphasis to enhance your appearance.

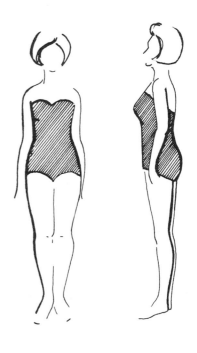

HIP-HEAVY   TOP-HEAVY

WEIGHT CHART

HEIGHT (without shoes)	SMALL FRAME st lb — st lb	MEDIUM FRAME st lb — st lb	LARGE FRAME st lb — st lb
4 ft 11 ins	6 10 — 7 3	7 0 — 7 12	7 8 — 8 10
5 ft 0 ins	6 13 — 7 6	7 3 — 8 1	7 11 — 8 13
5 ft 1 ins	7 1 — 7 9	7 6 — 8 4	8 0 — 9 2
5 ft 2 ins	7 4 — 7 12	7 9 — 8 7	8 3 — 9 5
5 ft 3 ins	7 7 — 8 1	7 12 — 8 10	8 6 — 9 8
5 ft 4 ins	7 10 — 8 4	8 1 — 9 0	8 9 — 9 12
5 ft 5 ins	7 13 — 8 7	8 4 — 9 4	8 13 — 10 2
5 ft 6 ins	8 2 — 8 11	8 8 — 9 9	9 3 — 10 6
5 ft 7 ins	8 8 — 9 1	8 12 — 9 13	9 7 — 10 10
5 ft 8 ins	8 10 — 9 5	9 2 — 10 3	9 11 — 11 0
5 ft 9 ins	9 0 — 9 9	9 6 — 10 7	10 1 — 11 4
5 ft 10 ins	9 4 — 10 0	9 10 — 10 11	10 5 — 11 9
5 ft 11 ins	9 8 — 10 4	10 0 — 11 1	10 9 — 12 0
6 ft 0 ins	9 12 — 10 8	10 4 — 11 5	10 13 — 12 5

THE SHORT FIGURE

If you are a perfectly proportioned, trim, small girl, enjoy the fact that this is the figure most men like. You can wear almost any style as long as it is correctly proportioned for you. Clear simple lines are best with no fuss or clutter for understated elegance.

The problem is that often the short girl is long-waisted with short legs. To appear taller and long-legged, aim at focusing attention on the upper part of the figure and thus creating an illusion of height. The trick is to make the figure look longer from waist to toe. Top interest on the bodice is good if not too bulky or heavy looking. Avoid clothes which cut the figure below the waistline and any style which has the tendency to swamp the figure. Choose ensembles — dresses and full-length coats rather than suits. One-colour garments will always give a trim appearance.

FABRICS
Dull-finished fabrics like crepe or lightweight wool are most suitable. Soft-coloured and small prints are in keeping with your size. Large printed designs and shiny fabrics do little to flatter and tend to overpower your small frame.

FOUNDATION GARMENTS
Choose an all-in-one garment for a smooth, long line. Never wear a foundation garment too long or one that breaks you at the waist, as neither will give a smooth silhouette.

If the bust is large enough for a bra without padding, choose one which has circular, stitched cups which will push up the bust and give more frontage. If some fullness is needed, select a bra with padding or firm shaping in the lower part of the cup for the required extra fullness. For a very small bust or an almost flat figure, invest in a bra with pre-formed cups and slightly thicker padding with under-bust wiring to give additional shaping.

DRESSES

Always stress the vertical with long, unbroken lines. Tucks, braids, vertical stripes, and buttons from neck to hem do miracles to add height. The most flattering dresses to wear are empire-, princess-, and A-line styles with bell or gored skirts. Sheath coat dresses give a tall slender silhouette. Do not clutter the garment with unnecessary detail and trimming. Avoid very full skirts and sudden flares below the hips, as well as tiered, trumpet, and tunic-line skirts, and very short skirts which give a no-leg look.

Wear detail on the bodice only. Deep V, low-scoop, and horseshoe neckline accentuate the length. High, muffling necklines and big collars shorten the neck and give a dumpy appearance.

Any length sleeve which is neat and uncluttered with cuffs kept in proportion to the tiny figure is suitable. Exaggerated and long vertical-striped sleeves distort the arms.

EVENING WEAR

A full-length gown with the bodice high in the front and with a low back is the most flattering to wear. The skirt can be flared and not too full. Short evening gowns emphasize short legs.

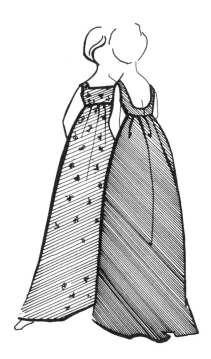

CASUAL WEAR

Casual dresses, skimmers, and empire-line shifts are suitable to all short figures. So are high-waisted skirts, slacks, and culottes. All-in-one playsuits, trouser-suits, and slacks worn with a shirt or top of the same or matching colour give the leggy look required. If shorts are worn, keep them very brief to show as much leg length as possible.

Bermuda-length shorts, knee-length socks and too many colours in casual wear will give a stunted appearance.

Bikinis are only for the well-proportioned small girl. One-piece swimsuits in one colour cut high on the sides without a skirt are best for the short girl who is not so well endowed. Beach parkas and sun-cover garments are ideal worn over any style of swimsuit for co-ordination.

SUITS

Wear jackets to the hipbone or waist only, or under-the-bust boleros.

Suits to avoid have long jackets, heavy shoulder padding, and details such as pockets below the waist. Never wear strong colour contrasts between the jacket and the skirt.

COATS

Full-length, slim, or princess-line coats enhance the figure. Tuxedo fronts and any vertical detail will give additional length to the figure.

Belted, short coats with big patch pockets or fur trim at the hemline are disaster to the short figure.

FURS

Wear fur trimming at the neck of a garment rather than a fur jacket or stole. If you want to wear a fur coat, select a full-length one cut on slim lines in a flat fur like sealskin, mole, or antelope.

Avoid thick chunky furs like chinchilla or long-haired ones like fox or snow leopard which will swamp your figure.

MILLINERY

Wear small hats which stress height—large ones will dwarf you. Look taller wearing turbans, pillboxes, flowerpot-shape hats, Tyrolean hats trimmed with high feathers, Bretons, pixie caps, high crowns, and turned-back, face-framing brims. You alone of all figure types can wear small caps to the most dashing effect. Wear an eye veil only.

Avoid downward sweeping brims and never wear an exaggerated line which will distort your figure. Do not wear head-hugging hoods, shoulder-length snoods, head scarves, or face-covering veils.

JEWELLERY

Wear little jewellery at any one time—just one piece worn high on the shoulder or a single, long-strand necklace. Small stud earrings and filigree jewellery will suit you. Do not overload yourself with large chunky jewellery or long drop earrings. This type of jewellery is strictly for the taller figures.

HANDBAGS

Use a full-length mirror to pick the correct size of handbag for your proportion. Choose colours to blend in with your clothes for that one-colour effect. Styling should be soft and feminine in antelope, grosgrain, satin, and other fabrics. Avoid large tailored, leather handbags which look like miniature briefcases. Strong contrast in colour for handbags gives a spotty look to the overall effect.

HOSIERY

Select stockings and tights in a colour to tone in with the skirt or shoe colouring. Contrast in stocking colour will break the leg length and divide the figure into the wrong proportions. Fancy, highly patterned stockings will draw attention to short legs.

SHOES

Low-cut, plain court shoes with medium to fairly high heels in a neutral colour will best tone in with the garment and stockings. Thong-style sandals with thin straps will give a bare look to the legs. Boots of any description, shoes which come high up on the instep, ornate trimming, and ankle strap fastenings make the legs appear too short.

THE TALL FIGURE

If you are slim, you can wear the extremes in fashion and get away with it. Be impressive and dramatic by dressing in bright, vibrant or light colours in big, bold prints. Choose unusual and large accessories to dwarf your height, and never be afraid of overdoing it. Use any detail to distract attention from the length. Do not slouch or droop the shoulders, nor stand with bended knees. All this does is to make you look self-conscious and ruins any effect created by elegant dressing.

Your problem often is a short body and long legs. The illusion is to make the figure appear longer from the neck to the waist by altering the proportions and by wearing a plain bodice with all the detail on the skirt to cut up the skirt area. Avoid wearing severely tailored, mannish clothes or styling which emphasizes vertical lines.

FABRICS

Any type of fabric can be worn—spots, checks, tartans, horizontal stripes, or prints with any size design.

FOUNDATION GARMENTS

Choose a deep, high-waisted girdle of the correct length. It must fit at the waist; if the girdle is too short it will put strain on the stockings and ladder them. Only buy a corselette if it is made to measure, as ordinary-sized ones are generally too short for an extra-long body. A well-constructed bra will make the most of your bosom.

DRESSES

Stress the horizontal with wide belts, skirts which are banded with different colours featuring trim detail. Dropped waist-line, hip drapes, peplums, paniers, and pockets all help break up the skirt area. Skirts that are bell, flared, gathered,

pleated, tiered, trumpet-line or fish-tail are the most flattering to the tall figure.

Bodices should be plain and uncluttered. Wear boat-shaped necks, wide, square or round face-framing necklines, and large collars.

Sleeves should be short or to the elbow or $\frac{3}{4}$-length, and must not cling to the arms. If the sleeves must be long, make them full and gathered into deep cuffs.

Avoid slim princess-lines, vertical stripes, or buttons, seams, tucks, and pleats from the neck to the hem. Avoid also anything that makes you look seven-foot tall by accentuating the vertical. Never wear long, skinny sleeves in knitted fabrics, as they give an ape-like appearance to the arms.

EVENING WEAR
Bare shoulders and necklines with short skirts are the most suitable for evening wear. Handkerchief and dipping hem-lines add interest. Full-length skirts must be full or shaped to give line. A printed or check skirt with a solid-colour bodice will break the length of the gown. Long, slim gowns in one colour should be worn only if the figure is striking.

CASUAL WEAR
Select exotic resort wear, vivid-printed sun clothes, patterned silk shirts worn outside skirts and pants, large bulky sweaters and cardigan-type jackets, and ski-sweaters with bold horizontal patterns. If trousers are to be worn, then pick straight or wide-legged ones, knee-length shorts worn with long socks, culottes or full harem pants and lounging pyjamas. Really brief shorts, long skinny trousers and tights are only attractive if the legs are well shaped.

Swimsuits can be strapless with hip interest, horizontal stripes, and with a skirt. Contrasting colours add interest to the design. Bikinis should be avoided because they give the appearance of a giraffe.

COATS
Wear big, bulky coats in checks, rough-textured fabrics, and combinations of different types of fabric. Styling is best with large pockets below the waist and low-slung belts in trench coat and raglan styles. The tall figure is the only type to successfully wear casual

jackets in different colours and fabrics without being swamped by bulkiness. Skinny coats with tuxedo fronts or braid from neck to hem are unflattering to the tall girl.

FURS
Sumptuous, long-haired furs such as fox, snow leopard, chinchilla and monkey fur are ideal in big fur collars, stoles, and jackets. Antelope trench coats, loosely belted with big deep pockets look well. Shun flat furs unless styled to add bulk to the figure. Mean little single fur ties add nothing to the appearance.

SUITS
The most flattering suits are those with longer jackets, belted casual styles with loose sleeves, and slight padding in the shoulders. Short, high-waisted jackets and bolero suits give the appearance of having grown out of the garment, and should not be worn.

ACCESSORIES
Millinery
Choose your millinery in perfect proportion to your height. Wear arresting shapes in daring colours with wide, large brims. A wide, flat sailor hat will save you an inch in height while a turned down brim saves two more inches. Hats worn at an angle, coolie hats, and wide fur hats look wonderful. Hats should never rise above the head. Do not wear high, pointed crowns and small, babyish caps as they will make you look pin-headed.

Jewellery
Jewellery can be flamboyant—large chunky bracelets, big splashy necklaces or chokers, clips and dress rings, jumbo-size stud earrings, large flowers, or a cluster of small flowers. Avoid wearing long necklaces down to the waist, small insignificant lapel ornaments and long dangling earrings.

Handbags
Handbags should be oversized, of square or pouchy shape in clutch or short-handle styles. Small handbags

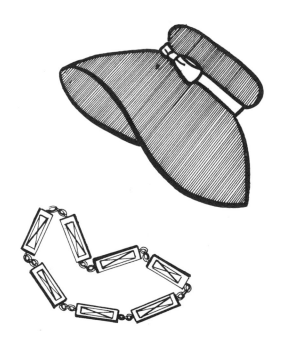

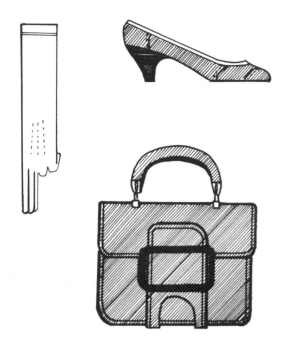

look as if you are carrying a child's bag by mistake. Shun shoulderstrap handbags which accentuate the height.

Gloves
Long and elbow-length gloves are ideal. For a shorter glove, push the longer ones down. Wrist-length gloves tend to give the appearance of growing out of them.

Shoes
Wear short, vamped shoes with either square or rounded toes. Medium-height heels are better than too high or flat. Open-toed and strapped sandals cut down at the side will foreshorten the length of the foot. Boots of any length are ideal for winter. Shoes to avoid are flatties or pointed toes which make your feet look longer.

THE ANGULAR FIGURE

The angular figure can wear to advantage the extreme of fashion from Paris which would be a disaster on other figure types. This figure type is the perfect "clothes horse" or high fashion model figure. The essential thing in dressing is not to emphasize the bones, but to conceal them by avoiding straight lines and too-tailored clothes which will make the boyish figure too masculine.

The problem of the angular figure is to conceal bone structure, which is part of thinness. The solution is to soften the outline and create the illusion of feminine curves by avoiding bare necklines and shoulders and clinging fabrics which hug the figure. The thin or angular girl can get away with becoming extra details and trimming which look fussy on a fuller figure. Avoid tailored accessories and select every accessory with an eye to femininity, bearing in mind that you are not the stark tailored type. Wear drapery, gathers, frills, pleats, shirring, tucks, and bows.

FABRICS
Fabrics should have body like velvet, taffeta, brocade, quilted satin, pleated sheers, embroidered silk, lace, tweed, mohair, terry towelling and big, bold prints. Avoid thin clinging jerseys and vertical stripes which make the figure look thinner. Light, bright colour helps to add width to the angular figure.

FOUNDATION GARMENTS
For the angular figure wear a bra with special inside shaping or moulding to give a high and more rounded look. Lightweight, seamless girdles should go to the waistline. Do not make the mistake of wearing a bra shell because the small bust requires some support. A brief suspender belt will cause the clothes to fall incorrectly and will show a ridge through the garment.

DRESSES

Choose clothes fitted in at the waist, wrist, and hips as these are the best assets of the angular figure. The skirt should bell out from a nipped-in waist to give grace. Skirts can be gathered, pleated, or tiered. A bodice falling from gently widened shoulders, softly over the bust to a tiny waist, will do a lot for a small bust Bodices can be cut with horizontal lines, draped, quilted, tucked, or frilled. Detail on bodices can make the garments.

Sheath, straight, figure-hugging dresses are not suitable to the figure type. Avoid the short, peg-top or hip-draped skirts which taper to a narrow hemline, as this draws attention to thin legs. This style of skirt can be worn only if full length, as the tapered line is not so acute and the legs are covered.

Wear high, covered necklines to avoid displaying the collar bones, salt cellars, and a skinny neck. During the day, high turtle or polo necklines or possibly Mandarin collars, high cowls, and ruffled necklines will show to advantage a long, slender neck. Sathed or rounded necklines add softness to a thin neck and face. Long pointed collars give an angular appearance and plunging necklines are unflattering. Off-the-shoulder or severely plain necklines should not be worn without relief of some sort of collar, drapery, or jewellery. Halter necklines cover the collar bones but leave bony shoulders exposed.

Long, full, soft sleeves fitted into the wrist will take away the effect of "pipe-cleaner" arms. You should cover the elbows where possible—even in summer—because they look ugly. A more tailored sleeve looks better pushed up, and cuffs take away that harsh look. It is unwise to wear long, tight sleeves and sleeveless dresses which will make too thin arms look bony.

EVENING WEAR

A full-length evening gown with a flared or full skirt gives elegance to the appearance. The angular figure type looks well in floating drapery, which should be worn tossed high at the neck and trailing out behind you. A cut-away neckline or a strapless bodice needs to be covered with lace or chiffon.

If you have thin legs it is unwise to wear short evening gowns. A strapless evening gown and low-backed garments would show prominent shoulder blades and collar bones. Slinky gowns need the necessary curves for the "femme fatale" look.

SUITS

Softly belted dressmaker suits will give rounded lines. Most flattering is a short, unfitted jacket with a flared or pleated skirt or a double-breasted jacket with a contrasting coloured skirt. Suits to avoid are the mannish, tailored suits with jigger buttoning, pointed lapels, and square shoulders designed on square cut lines.

COATS

Wear capes, coachman-style greatcoats, or raglan-sleeved, belted trenchcoats with large pockets and wide, rounded shoulders. Fitted coats should be loose with a flared skirt to suggest the figure rather than reveal it. For this type of coat, stress the horizontal lines with either empire-line or a waist or hip seam. Avoid box jackets and tuxedo-front coats which have narrow shoulders and skinny sleeves.

FURS

Fur capes and jackets will give fullness to the figure. Fur ties worn high at the throat will soften a thin neck. Touches of fur trim on clothes will flatter the figure. Fur should be exquisitively soft and long haired-chinchilla, sable, and fox are perfect. Fur-lined hoods make an attractive frame for the face.

CASUAL WEAR

Most flattering to wear are bulky mohair sweaters a size larger than usual, vibrant, soft silk blouses, wide-leg trousers, trouser-suits, culottes, flowing hostess-type lounge pyjamas, full-length patio skirts, and thick, gathered wool skirts.

Wear swimsuits that cover as much of the figure as possible with pleated or gathered skirts and wide straps. Choose a swimsuit with a matching coat, a bulky terry-towelling parka, or a loose covering for glamour when not actually swimming.

Never wear shorts which reveal stork-like legs or Bermuda-length shorts which display knobbly knees. Bare midriffs show a prominent rib cage, and bikinis reveal the skeleton rather than the figure. Tight, clinging sweaters only emphasize a flat chest.

ACCESSORIES

Millinery

Soft little hats trimmed with flowers, ribbons, or provocative veils will enhance the face. Toques, "squashy" berets, bretons, coolie, fur, or any hat with a soft line will flatter. Do not wear tailored and flat sailor hats with stark styling or high, pointed crowns or hats which give a beak-like look to a slim face.

Jewellery

Select feminine designs with gem stones in antique or filigree setting, bibs of jewelled mesh, multistrands of pearls, and beads or deep chokers. Wide bracelets will give slender hands and wrists a fragile look. Do not wear single-strand, low-hanging pearls, or beads which do absolutely nothing for the appearance.

Gloves

Gloves should be in soft fabrics ending between the elbow and the wrist, and worn pushed down into soft folds. Do not wear wrist-length gloves, as they make the wrist and arms look thinner.

Handbags

Handbags should be softly shaped and "bunchy" looking in suede, antelope, velvet, or other feminine fabrics. Do not carry the traditional lizard or crocodile bag because the shape is not feminine enough.

Hosiery

Wear light-coloured, dull-finished stockings and tights to give the calf more shape.

Shoes

Wear higher-heeled, short, vamped shoes with rounded or square toes with cut-outs, toe caps, and any design detail or trim. Pointed-toe shoes are the wrong style for the angular figure, which usually has long, slender feet. Boots of any description are leg flattering.

THE HEAVY FIGURE

The figure problem of this type is all-over heaviness, and clothes must be selected to trim the figure. Wear clothes which flow away from the figure and fit easily. Avoid clinging garments which mould the contours too closely and emphasize the bulk. Colours should be muted, neutral, or dark to give a neater, softer silhouette. Vivid or light colours make you look larger and more conspicuous.

Too small a garment will suggest that you have gained weight or that the garment has shrunk. Buy a size larger; only you will see the size tab—everyone else will see the final result. If the legs are heavy, wear the skirt a little longer than the current fashionable length.

FABRIC

Wear dull-finish silks, crepes, fine wools, and small, misty all-over prints. Keep to muted or soft, clear colours, depending on hair, eyes, and skin colouring. Avoid any fabric which adds weight— for example, tweed and long-haired or heavy-pile fabrics. Satins and lamés will highlight every curve you have. Do not wear large spots or checks, big bold prints, or horizontal stripes.

FOUNDATION GARMENTS

Invest in really good quality foundation garments to control and support the figure and to give a trim appearance. An all-in-one foundation garment gives the best result because it prevents a bulge over the girdle and controls a flabby diaphragm. It is essential that this type of garment is personally fitted. If separate garments are preferred, then select a high-waisted girdle with an extra-firm control panel over the tummy and tail. Wide straps will prevent shoulder cutting.

Throw out foundation garments immediately they do not supply the control needed; otherwise they will emphasize your figure faults. Garments which are too lightweight or short will not give proper support, although a correctly fitted foundation need not be heavy and uncomfortable.

Always wear a slip under dresses and suits; otherwise the clothes will cling in a most undesirable manner.

DRESSES

Dresses should have unbroken lines from shoulder to hem. Vertical lines accentuate the height and take away the width. Remember that stripes, pleats, tucks, decorative seams, and rows of buttons emphasize the direction in which they travel. Endeavour to dress slim at all times.

Wear shirtmaker and coat-style dresses. Necklines should not be too high to lose neck length or too low to show cleavage. V-necks are the most flattering. Avoid wearing full-gathered skirts, hip drapery, fussy detail, and tight, clinging dresses.

Skirts should be gently flared or gored from the hip, or with pleats at the centre, front, or back. Subtly indicate the waistline, and rely on the flare of the skirt and slightly wider shoulder to convey a small waist by contrast.

Short and ¾-length sleeves are the most flattering. Loose arm-holes make the upper arms appear smaller. Skin-tight sleeves make you look as if you have muscles, and sleeveless garments emphasize the heavy upper arm.

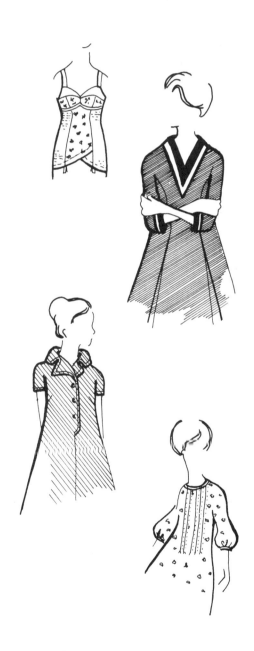

EVENING WEAR

Choose full-length evening gowns in one colour only. Flared and gored skirts are more attractive to the heavy figure than gathered skirts. Slim skirts will restrict movement when dancing. If your shoulders are good, wear wide, interesting necklines. Cover heavy upper arms with sleeves or drapery. Wear a full-length evening coat rather than a jacket or a stole. Short, fussy evening gowns are never flattering to the heavy figure.

SUITS

Wear dresses and coats rather than suits. These are more slimming and more flattering. The best jacket length for a suit is mid-hip. Wear swagger styles and designs featuring vertical seams. If double-breasted buttoning is required, keep the buttons close together and of the same colour as the garment. Contrasting colours in jackets and skirts should be avoided. Any multicolour combination will emphasize heaviness.

COATS

Wear full-length coats at all times. These should be styled on slim lines, accentuating vertical detail. Match the coat with the colour of the dress to give a co-ordinated ensemble. Deep, muted colours are more suitable than harsh, bright colours. Avoid wearing any type of short coat, especially in checks or contrasting colours. Do not fully belt a coat unless wanting a heavier look. Deep-pile fabrics also contribute to bulk.

FURS

Fur coats are not generally flattering to the heavier figure They add bulk which must be avoided at all times if trying to achieve a trimmer silhouette. If furs must be worn, select a flat, sleek skin such as antelope or seal in styles similar to the coats. Fur hats and trimmings must be selected with great care.

CASUAL WEAR

Casual separates should be the same colour or just a tone deeper if unable to match the colour exactly. Shirts or blouses should be worn outside the other garments. If blouses are to be worn tucked-in, they must be tapered and darted to take away the bunchy look. Buy sweaters a size larger; men's are ideal because the styling is generally classic and uncluttered.

Tailored trouser-suits will give a trim appearance only if the jacket is long enough to cover the tail. Great attention must be given to the correct fit of trousers and slacks. The legs should be wide enough not to emphasize the size of the hips. For casual wear, gored culottes are very suitable as they give the same freedom of movement as trousers and have the neatness of a dress. Never wear shorts. For ski-ing, match the colour of the trousers with that of the sweater and parka.

Swim wear should be the classic, plain swimsuit in one colour devoid of any fussy trim. A dress-length beach cover is more advisable than a short one as it will hide heavy thighs.

ACCESSORIES

Accessories must be kept in proportion to figure size. These should be classic in styling for a truly elegant appearance. All the accessories must be considered with the ensemble before purchasing. This is particularly important when buying a hat.

Millinery

Wear eye-catching hats. These can be worn at any angle if suitable. Width above the brow line will help off-set heavy hip width. Flat and tiny hats make you look moon-faced. Do not wear turbans unless they are high, bold, and bulky. Avoid turned-down brims, as they hide any neck you have.

Jewellery

Jewellery should be large and simple in styling, with refined settings for gemstones. Dress clips and brooches should be worn high on the shoulder to detract from an ample bosom. Graduated pearls will give added neck length. Wide chokers will lose any neck you have. Wide bracelets and dress rings make the hands look fatter. Stud earrings are the only style that really flatter the face. Avoid long, dangling beads and earrings, or you will look like a walking bazaar.

Belts

Wear narrow, self-fabric belts. Half-belts which do not encircle you are most attractive. Dull calf or suede belts which tone with the garment are preferable to shiny patent leather. Contrasting-coloured belts draw attention to a thick waistline. Never wear a belt pulled too tight. Wide belts create bulges, and elastic belts give a "sack of potatoes" look to the garment and figure.

Gloves

Long and ¾-length plain-styled gloves are the most elegant. Wrist-length gloves make the hands look fat and stumpy. Elaborate and fancy gloves give a cluttered look to the overall appearance.

Handbags

Larger handbags make you look smaller by comparison. Styles must be unadorned to be attractive. The small, dolly-size handbags and ones trimmed with eye catching clasps and gilt frames are to be avoided.

Hosiery

Dull-finished stockings and tights in a darker tone than fashion decrees will give the illusion of slimness to the legs. The larger figure still requires the additional support of a girdle even with tights.

Shoes

Wear plain, court shoes with medium-height heels a tone darker than your clothes. Stilt heels make you appear to totter. You need a wider, lower heel as a firm base to balance the bulk above.

THE HIP-HEAVY FIGURE

If your bust measurement is well under your hip measurement, then your figure is classed as hip-heavy. Often the legs are more solid than average, and the figure proportions need to be re-arranged to give the appearance of a slimmer hipline. Focus attention above the waist with eye-catching detail and interesting necklines.

FOUNDATION GARMENTS

Choose a girdle to give a long, smooth line and firm control, particularly at the back and front. Avoid foundation garments which are too lightweight to give proper control. Wear a bra with a good up-lift to prevent a short-waisted look. Never wear a bra which is too soft for support.

SUITS

Suits with loose jackets or bolero-length tops with neck interest are ideal. Jackets fitted tightly at the waistline will emphasize the wide hips. Any styling detail which ends at the hipline is out.

ACCESSORIES

Millinery

Wear gay hats with brim width which will balance the hip measurements. Hats to avoid are close-fitting, small hats. These will make you look narrow at the top or pin-headed, and draw attention to the hipline.

Handbags and Gloves

Medium-size, simply shaped handbags in either envelope or short-handled styles are the most elegant. Dangling, long-handled, little handbags, and short, stubby umbrellas do precisely nothing for your appearance.

Choose basic, plain gloves which will blend in colour with your clothes. Remember that short, fancy gloves with frills and trims lead the eye back to the hips.

Hosiery

Choose darker-toned, fine-denier stockings or tights for a more slender effect. Thick, heavy, light-coloured stockings give the legs a more solid look. Avoid fancy, eye-catching stockings and long socks.

Shoes

Medium-heeled shoes should be worn in a colour which blends in with the apparel. Heavy, thick-heeled shoes give a clumsy appearance to the feet and ankles. Bright, contrasting colours and highly trimmed shoes take attention from the neckline to focus on rather solid legs.

DRESSES.

Easy-fitting, simply styled dresses with flared or gored skirts will trim the hipline. Dark skirts worn with lighter-coloured bodices or blouses will re-arrange your proportions by visibly slimming the hips. Skirts worn slightly longer than fashion decrees will help to flatter this figure type. Interesting necklines, detail on the bodice, jewellery worn high on the shoulder, and colourful scarves will attract the eye away from the hips.

Avoid wearing tight, tapered skirts or full, bunchy ones. Pleated skirts, hip drapery, or dropped waistlines add width. Fancy belts of any description, especially pulled in tight, make the waist look small but the hips much wider.

TOP-HEAVY FIGURE

The problem of the top-heavy figure is that the body is too heavy above the waistline for the slimmer part below. This figure is often referred to as a Continental figure, and often has slender hips with slim ankles and legs. The balance or proportion has to be re-distributed to avoid the "pouter pigeon" or top-heavy look. To do this it is essential to keep the interest of the design near the face or below waist-level, avoiding bulk at the bodice and detail at the bustline.

FOUNDATION GARMENTS

The correct foundation garments are most important with first consideration to the choosing of the right type of bra to give the required firm support and uplift. The cup must fit perfectly, and a longer bra will do most for this figure. Wider stretch straps will prevent shoulder cutting. Avoid short-length, low-cut bras which offer inadequate underneath support.

DRESSES

Dresses are best in all-over dark colours with unadorned neckline. A narrow V-neckline is an excellent choice. All lines on the bodice must be vertical to create a slender look, with softly rounded shoulders which give a tapered effect at the waistline. Loose ¾-length sleeves are more flattering than sleeveless garments or sleeves which are tightly fitted or puffed. Skirts flaring out at the hem, pleats, or fullness from a dropped waistline all help in the illusion. Never wear a tight, clinging bodice with excess trimming, draping, or fussiness on the bodice; it only emphasizes the bustline.

SUITS

Suits should have long, loose cardigan-style jackets with narrow lapels rather than those fitted into the waist. Raglan sleeves give a rounded shoulder line, while excess shoulder padding gives the appearance of a weightlifter. Wide, double-breasted buttoning on a jacket will broaden the figure where it is not required. If you are of average height or tall, then wear a dark jacket with light-coloured skirts. A navy blazer-jacket with a white, pleated skirt will re-distribute the proportions.

ACCESSORIES

Millinery

Eye-catching, small, or medium-size face-framing hats worn at an angle or with side-interest trimmings are more attractive than large hats with turned-down brims or tight turbans and tiny little hats.

Jewellery

Wear necklaces that sit at the base of the throat. Long, dangling ropes of beads or pearls are not for you as they have a tendency to swing-out over the prominent bustline. For greater impact, wear an attractive lapel ornament or brooch set close to the throat.

Shoes

If the ankles are slim, any style can be worn with distinction. Avoid stilt heels which give the figure a tottering look.

Handbags

Depending on figure size, carry a neat, medium-size or large handbag.

FACE FLATTERY

ROUND

LONG

SQUARE

HEART-SHAPED

The most perfect shape for a face is the classic oval, which very few women have. The four main face shapes are round, long, square, or heart-shaped. Face shapes do not necessarily go with figure types—a round face does not mean a heavy or plump figure. Through correct use of cosmetics and flattering hair-styles, any shape of face can achieve the illusion of perfection.

There are simple rules for flattering the face. Where the face is widest, keep the hair smooth or swept away, and widen the hair at the narrowest part of the face; a fringe shortens the shape while a centre parting lengthens the face and the nose. Thin faces need soft hairstyles, heavy features require loose, flowing lines— never curls. Do not wear a hairstyle just because it is the latest fashion. Try a flattering adaptation of the fashion by wearing the hair a little longer or shorter, the hair ends turned up or under to give you a more individual hairstyle.

THE ROUND FACE
The round face is often short and broad, with rounded contours and full cheeks. This shape requires lengthening, with height added to the crown of the head.

Wear high, narrow hairstyles with a side parting. Keep the side hair smooth and close to the head to minimize face roundness and to narrow the cheeks. Fringes brushed to the side and softness on the cheeks will break up the circular lines. Avoid tight, flat-topped, off-the-face hairstyles which emphasize the fullness of the face and the width of the cheeks.

Wear a hat with height, and try for width above the browline. Hats worn at an angle are flattering,

while pudding-basin and small hats make you appear all face.

Choose deep, plain neckline for slimness and length. High, round necklines and close-fitting collars must be avoided.

THE LONG FACE
If your face is long and thin with a narrow forehead, jawline, and cheekbones, the effect needed is fullness to the face.

The ideal hairstyle is of medium length with up-turned ends. The crown should be rounded with little or no height, and a full or part fringe used to shorten the features. Avoid wearing high, upswept styles or hair combed severely back to leave the brow bare.

Choose flat-topped millinery which will round the face. A beret or a coolie-shaped hat will give width at the sides. Do not wear small, fitted hats which make the face appear longer.

Wear necklines high and wide to give the necessary horizontal lines. Deep V-necklines and long, dangling bead or pendant earrings will accentuate the face length.

THE SQUARE FACE
If your face is square with the forehead and jawline of about equal width, the lines of the face must be softened to avoid emphasizing the awkward angles.

Choose soft hairstyles with an off-centre or diagonal parting, soft fringes, or waves over the brow with curls flicking out onto the cheeks. Height at the crown of the head with the hair long enough to softly taper at the

| ROUND | LONG | SQUARE | HEART-SHAPED |

sides makes the jawline appear slender. Do not wear a centre parting, straight fringe, flat-topped styles, or hair cut to widen out the jawline.

Wear a softly shaped hat with no angular lines. The brim of any hat should be wider than your jawline. Avoid wearing small hats, which will accentuate a prominent jaw.

Wide, round necklines (wider than the jawline) will take away the square look. Avoid at all cost square necklines and angular collars.

THE HEART-SHAPED FACE

The heart-shaped face has a wide forehead tapering down to a narrow jawline, often ending in pointed chin. Fullness is needed at the jaw level to counterbalance width at the temples.

The hair should be medium to long and looped over the forehead from a side parting, with a half-fringe which will take away some of the width from the forehead. Flick the hair out from the cheeks and jawline. Too much width at the temples will make the face appear wider and give the cheeks and chin a more tapered look.

Wear sou'wester hats and berets. Select hats with brims which are widest at the chin. Do not wear hats which are too high or too flat, small, or close-fitting to the top of the head.

To give the chin a shorter and more rounded appearance, wear shallow scoop-necklines. Avoid long, deep V-necklines which will accentuate the pointed chin.

GLASSES

These days glasses change fashion as often as other accessories, and if selected in the most flattering shape can be most becoming and enhance the face. Choose both the frame and hairstyle to suit your face shape. Avoid fancy and jewelled frames; they are not elegant and limit wear.

When wearing glasses, great care must be taken in choosing a hat. Avoid trying to cover glasses with drop-brimmed hats; select ones with more flattering, upsweeping brims.

Round face	Pick a squarish frame which is wider than the broadest part of the cheeks, and with narrow lenses to slim down the face.
Long face	For a shortening effect, wear deep lenses with wide-swept frames.
Square face	To soften facial contours, wear narrow, upswept frames at least as wide as the broadest part of the face, thus distracting from the squareness of the jaw.
Heart-shaped face	To add balance to a narrow chin, wear broad lenses set in uptilted frames which will soften the width of the forehead.

Motorbike Racing

Tony Norman

INSIDE STORY

Copyright © ticktock Entertainment Ltd 2006
First published in Great Britain in 2006 by ticktock Media Ltd,
Unit 2, Orchard Business Centre, North Farm Road,
Tunbridge Wells, Kent TN2 3XF

ISBN 1 86007 846 X

Printed in China

Picture credits (t=top; b=bottom; c=centre; l=left; r=right):
22B Action Images/Lee Mills Livepic; 15T Ducati;
6B Castrol Motor Oil; 24T, 25T, 25BL, 27BR Yamaha;
5TL, 7T, 9T, 16, 17T, 26B, 27T Red Bull

Every effort has been made to trace the copyright holders, and we
apologise in advance for any unintentional omissions. We would be
pleased to insert the appropriate acknowledgements in any subsequent
edition of this publication.

Neither the publishers nor the author shall be liable for any bodily harm
or damage to property whatsoever that may be caused or sustained as
a result of conducting any of the activities featured in this book.

Contents

INTRODUCTION   4-5

WHAT THE RACERS WEAR   6-7

MOTOCROSS   8-9

MOTOGP   10-11

RACE THE WORLD   12-13

SUPERBIKES   14-15

FREESTYLE JUMPS   16-17

SPEEDWAY   18-19

IT TAKES TWO   20-21

FACE THE FEAR   22-23

THE HALL OF FAME   24-25

RED HOT RACERS   26-27

AROUND THE WORLD   28-29

GLOSSARY   30-31

INDEX   32

Introduction

Motorbike racing is exciting and there are many different competitions for fans to enjoy. In MotoGP and superbike races, riders hit speeds of over 320 kph (200 mph). Motocross events are held on muddy tracks. Speedway bikes have no brakes. The rules may vary, but all riders have a fierce will to win.

EARLY DAYS

In 1867, American Sylvester Howard Roper made an early type of motorbike driven by steam that went 'faster than a horse'. The first motorbike driven by petrol was invented in Germany in 1885. It was made of wood and had a top speed of 11 kph (7 mph).

HOW THEY WORK

Motorbikes are powered by a piston inside a cylinder. Fuel is burnt to drive the piston up and down. The piston turns a shaft, which goes to the gearbox. The gearbox drives a chain that turns the rear wheel of the bike. The size of the cylinder is measured in cc (cubic centimetres). The bigger the cylinder, the more powerful the bike.

During a sidecar race, the passenger changes position often to help keep the motorbike stable.

RACING FACTS – DID YOU KNOW?

The first known motorbike race was held in 1894. The race was from Paris to Rouen, a distance of 128km (80 miles). The winner had an average speed of 16 kph (10 mph).

MOTOGP

SUPERBIKES

FREESTYLE

SPEEDWAY

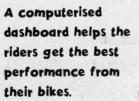
A computerised dashboard helps the riders get the best performance from their bikes.

To take a corner quickly, the rider leans into it.

What the Racers Wear

Motorbike racing takes many forms. The bikes change from sport to sport, but most riders wear the same sort of safety wear.

HELMET

The helmet must fit snugly on the head for safety. Full-face helmets give riders cover all round the head. A visor pulls down at the front of the helmet to protect the eyes. In some motorcycle sports, riders wear goggles.

Motorbike racers always wear special protection to minimize risk.

LEATHERS AND GLOVES

Motorbike riders wear leather because it is strong and gives good protection. Road leathers are sewn using a single row of stitches. Racing leathers are sewn with two or three rows for extra strength. It helps to stop the clothing splitting open in an accident. Leather gloves protect the hands and give a good grip to steer the bike. They are lightweight, flexible and strong.

BOOTS

Racing boots are tough and cover the feet and ankles. Boot soles are quite thin, so riders can feel how the bike below them is performing.

Motorbike gloves are long and go over the wrists of the leathers.

RACING FACTS - DID YOU KNOW?

Riders have to wear a name tag during races. This is so medical teams will know who they are in the event of a crash.

Knee guards are sometimes worn to provide extra protection.

TRUE STORIES

The film star Ewan McGregor is a motorbike racing fan. He rode his own motorbike round the world in 2004. The trip took 15 weeks and Ewan drove 32,000 km (20,000 miles).

Leathers come in several thicknesses and many colours.

A helmet's outer shell is made from plastic or fibreglass.

Motocross

Motocross is also known as MX or dirt bike racing. Riders race on a cross-country track of mud or sand. The tracks are about 1.5 km (one mile) long. MX bikes are light to help the riders twist round tight bends and jump over hills on the rough, open track.

RULES OF THE GAME

Up to 40 riders race to come home first over a set time, or number of laps. Each race is called a moto. There are usually two or three races on one day and the rider who is best overall wins.

SUPERMOTO AND SUPERCROSS

Supermoto is a cross between motocross and road racing. Most of the race is on tarmac, but some of it is cross-country. Supercross is a newer sport. The man-made tracks have steep, high jumps. Riders can soar 9 metres (30 feet) in the air during a race. About 25 riders take part in each race.

Motocross riders must be on top form over the whole event, not just one race.

Supercross competitions usually take place in a sports arena.

RACING FACTS – DID YOU KNOW?

Falls are bound to happen. A motocross bike is specially designed so the exhaust and pedals aren't damaged when it is dropped.

Shock absorbers help motocross bikes to land smoothly from high jumps.

Motocross engines are designed for quick acceleration, not top speed.

MX tyres have a thick tread to help grip the mud or sand on the track.

ı MotoGP

MotoGP is short for Motorcycle Grand Prix, or big prize. Races are held in countries all over the world. Riders travel to take part in these events and win points. The season runs for about seven months. The person with the most points at the end becomes **World Champion.**

HISTORY

MotoGP racing started in 1949. The best rider in history is Italy's Giacomo Agostini who won 122 Grand prix races and 15 world championship titles during the 60s and 70s.

TODAY'S STARS

The best MotoGP racer in recent years is Italy's Valentino Rossi. He won the MotoGP world crown three times in a row from 2002 to 2004. Other top riders include Alex Barros of Brazil, Max Biaggi of Italy, plus Nicky Hayden, Colin Edwards and Kenny Roberts, all of the USA.

MotoGP supporters come to see the best riders on the best bikes. The atmosphere is great.

A good start gives the rider a boost in the race ahead.

RACING FACTS - DID YOU KNOW?

Bikes are rated by the size of the engine cylinder, measured in cc (cubic centimetres). MotoGP now allows 990cc bikes, and new speed records are being set.

125cc is the smallest engine used in MotoGP.

TRUE STORIES

Max Biaggi grew up in Rome, Italy, dreaming of being a soccer star. Then a friend took him to a motorcycle race – and the rest is history. Max became the 250cc World Champion four times in a row between 1994 and 1997.

Until 1994, the most powerful bike used was 500cc.

In 2002, new rules allowed 990cc bikes to compete.

Race the World

There are three ways to be a MotoGP racer. Most young riders learn with races for 125cc bikes. The best riders move up to the next level, 250cc racing. The final jump is to top level MotoGP racing, with bikes of up to 990cc and speeds of over 320 kph (200 mph).

TOP TEAMS

Some of the top MotoGP teams are sponsored by Yamaha, Honda, Ducati and Suzuki. Riders work closely with the factory team who make their bike. Riders also trust their mechanics to make their bikes run at top speed.

HOW TO WIN

A good rider reaches top speed on the straight parts of the track, braking at the last possible moment for the corners. In close races, bikes are just inches apart. Winning a race takes courage and control.

Top riders see the bike ahead as a challenge, not a sign of defeat.

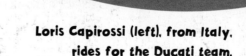

Loris Capirossi (left), from Italy, rides for the Ducati team.

RACING FACTS - DID YOU KNOW?

During a race, MotoGP riders can have no more than eight crew working on the bike. For races with 125cc and 250cc bikes, that drops to six.

Assen, France
Track length:
5.9 km (3.7 miles)

TRUE STORIES

Brazil's Alex Barros has been a MotoGP rider since 1990. Today he reaches speeds of 320 kph (200 mph), but Alex started by racing on mopeds at top speeds of 48 kph (30 mph)!

Motegi, Japan
Track length:
4.8 km (2.9 miles)

Jerez, Spain
Track length:
4.4 km (2.7 miles)

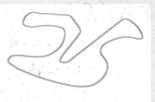

Freestyle Jumps

High jumps are part of FMX (Freestyle Motocross). The rider speeds up a 2.5 metre (8 feet) tall ramp and takes off at about 50 kph (30 mph) across a gap up to 27 metres (90 feet) wide. The motorbike (125cc or 250cc) flies 9–15 metres (30–50 feet) high in the air. The rider has under five seconds to do a mid-air stunt, before landing on the other side.

WINNERS

Five judges rate the riders in FMX ramp to ramp contests. They give the most points to riders who do difficult stunts with ease and style. The hardest stunt is a backflip, where the bike does a full 360° backflip in mid-air.

NEW TRICKS

Riders use foam pits to try out new mid-air stunts. The foam pit is a safe landing area filled with strips of foam. Riders take off from a ramp and practise their stunt. If the trick goes wrong, the rider and bike have a soft place to land.

A mid-air one hander.

RACING FACTS - DID YOU KNOW?

Las Vegas, 2003. American Ryan Capes made the longest motorbike jump ever. Ryan left the ramp at 115 kph (72 mph), and jumped his 250cc bike 79 metres (260 feet).

Tommy Clowers at the 2005 Red Bull Adventure Festival. Tommy is credited with adding new flourishes to many tricks.

An FMX rider pulls his bike on its side for this mid-air stunt called a tabletop.

TRUE STORIES

Ramp to ramp motorbike jumps are not new. American stunt rider Evel Knievel jumped 50 cars in 1973. In 1976, he crashed trying to jump a tank of sharks!

A no hander.

A no handed Indian Air (a move where the legs make a scissor-like kicking motion)

Speedway

Speedway bikes bear little resemblance to road-going motorbikes. They have no brakes and no suspension, and are designed to be very lightweight.

SPEEDWAY MEETS

There are many different classes of race at a speedway meet. In the top-rated Elite League there are 15 races every season. Speedway riders have two or more different bikes they can use. Their own mechanic travels with them to each race to looks after the bike. If it goes wrong, there may be only minutes to fix it before the next race. Mechanics work in an area called the pits, which is beside the track.

BARE BONES

Speedway racing is not for the fainthearted. To turn corners, the rider slides the back wheel sideways. Because there are no brakes, it is easy to make a mistake. Riders frequently hit the walls, the gravel track and other bikes. But the sport is huge fun!

In British speedway races, the 'home team' wear red and blue helmets.

When turning corners, new speedway riders balance themselves by putting a foot on the ground.

RACING FACTS - DID YOU KNOW?

Speedway riders can travel 80,500 km (50,000 miles) a year.
They drive to matches in vans with their bikes and mechanics.
Some vans are very luxurious, with beds, a TV and a fridge.

Top speedway riders tend to be short and lightweight with lots of stamina.

TRUE STORIES

The Australian Jason Crump finished in second place in the 2001, 2002 and 2003 speedway world championships. In 2004 he finally succeeded in winning the title.

Speedway tracks are usually about 0.8 km (0.5 miles) long.

It Takes Two

Sidecars have one wheel and are attached to the side of a motorbike. They have space for one passenger. The motorbikes with sidecars that take part in races are known simply as sidecars. They look very different from the motorbikes and sidecars seen on the roads.

There are 16 races during the World Championship season. Drivers compete for points.

INCHES ABOVE THE TRACK

Sidecar racing first became popular in the 1920s but the first MotoGP sidecar races took place in 1949. Passengers have a vital role to play during a race. They must lean towards or away from the motorbike to stabilize the vehicle around bends and allow it to go faster.

SUPER POWER

Sidecars competing in World Championships have the same 1000cc engines as superbikes. Car and bike have a single aluminium chassis (frame). The three wheels are small with a thick tyre. These advanced racing machines are more like racing cars than motorcycles.

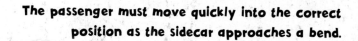

The passenger must move quickly into the correct position as the sidecar approaches a bend.

RACING FACTS - DID YOU KNOW?

One of the world's best sidecar teams is made up of two brothers. British racers Tim and Tristan Reeves say that knowing each other well helps them to win races.

The aerodynamic design of a sidecar helps it go faster.

 It's a thrilling ride for driver and passenger, sitting just centimetres above the track.

 Passengers must hold on tightly. Sometimes a  passenger loses his grip and is thrown out of the sidecar.

The Hall of Fame

The top motorbike riders are heroes to their fans.

VALENTINO ROSSI

Rossi won his first title in Italy in 1994 at the age of 15. He won the 125cc world championship in 1997, and went on to become the youngest 250cc world champ. In 2002 he won his first MotoGP world crown. Rossi always wears the number 46, the same number as his father, who also was a MotoGP racer.

MICK DOOHAN

The best Australian MotoGP racer ever. Mick won the 500cc World Championship five times in a row, 1994-98. Mick loved taking part in tough races with other top riders. He had to retire after a crash in Spain, but he is still seen as a hero of the track.

KENNY ROBERTS

One name, two generations of American heroes. Kenny Roberts senior had some great races and won the 1978 500cc MotoGP world championship. Kenny held the title for the next two years. Kenny's son, Kenny junior, then won the same crown in 1999.

Valentino Rossi is already considered one of the greatest MotoGP riders of all time.

RACING FACTS – DID YOU KNOW?

In 1937, the world speed record for motorbikes was 278 kph (173 mph). In 2004, John Noonan, from California, recorded the fastest ever speed on a motorbike – 397 kph (246.8 mph).

Noriyuki Haga from Japan is the top rider for the Yamaha World Superbike team.

TRUE STORIES

England's John Surtees won seven motorbike world titles in the 1950s. John then switched to Formula One racing cars in 1960 and became world champ in that sport too!

The Swedish speedway rider Tony Rickardsson has won the World Championship six times.

Kenny Roberts is one of the great heroes of MotoGP.

Red Hot Racers

Motorbike racing takes many forms. MX bikes twist and jump over cross-country tracks. Speedway stars race on bikes with no brakes. MotoGP stars ride a new track every two weeks of the season. Superbikes race at over 200 mph. Top riders share one thing: the skill they show in the heat of the race.

DOING IT RIGHT

Crashes and even death are part of motorbike racing. Accidents do happen. The best riders are extremely competitive, but follow the racing rules to minimize the injuries from accidents. Sponsors expect their riders to follow high standards and win fairly.

RACING ALL OVER THE WORLD

Riders from all over the world enjoy high-speed races in the 21st century. This is an international sport. Things have come a long way since the first motorbike rode down the road at 11 kph (7 mph)!

Professional or amateur, motorbike racers enjoy talking about their sport with other competitors.

To win a motocross race a rider needs control as well as speed.

RACING FACTS - DID YOU KNOW?

Squid live in the sea, right? Wrong. In MX racing, a 'squid' is a rider who can't control the bike and sways around like the arms of a squid.

The riders focus their minds on winning as they line up at the start of a speedway race.

TRUE STORIES

Japan's Shinji Kazama set a new world record in 1987, when he became the first person to ride to the North Pole on a motorbike.

The machines used in superbike racing are modified versions of bikes available to buy.

Rossi in the lead at the 2005 MotoGP race in Sachsenring, Germany.

Around the World

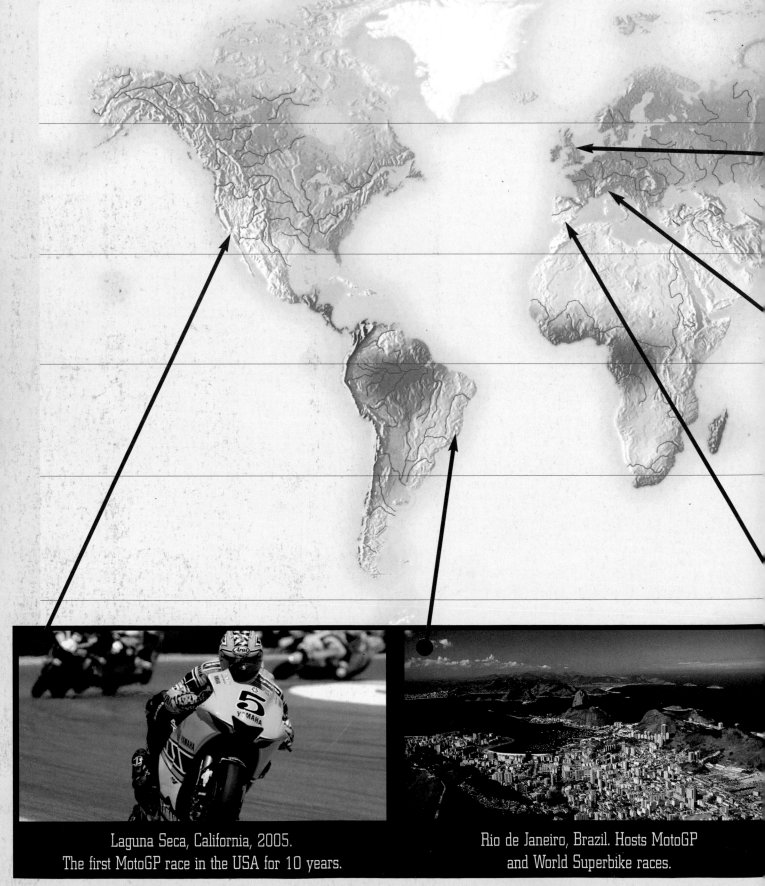

Laguna Seca, California, 2005.
The first MotoGP race in the USA for 10 years.

Rio de Janeiro, Brazil. Hosts MotoGP
and World Superbike races.

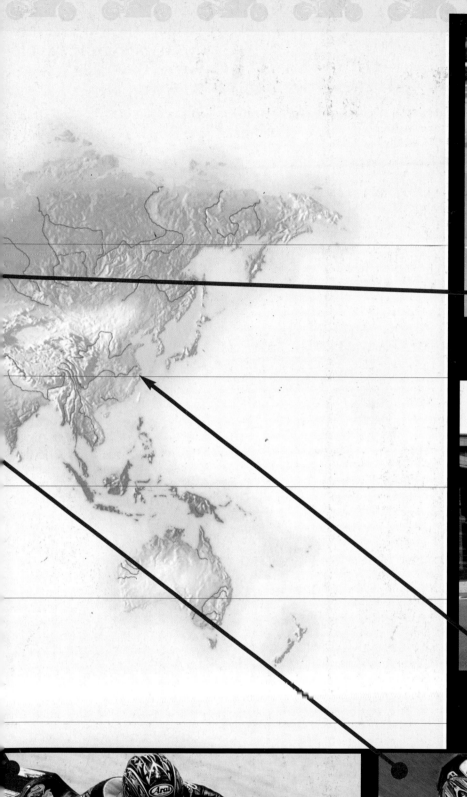

The TT race on the Isle of Man, UK.

Shanghai, China. One of the latest and best MotoGP tracks.

Jerez, Spain. Crowds of over 120,000 watch MotoGP racing here.

Monza, Italy. Famous track. Hosts MotoGP, World Superbikes and F1 car racing.

Glossary

Acceleration
An increase in speed of a vehicle produced by pressing the gas pedal (accelerator).

Aerodynamics
The science of designing machines to slip through the air more easily. This helps them to go faster. Slim, smooth shapes are better than shapes with corners or angles.

Chassis
The metal framework of a motor vehicle. The body and working parts of the vehicle are attached to the chassis. A sidecar is built on a chassis.

Engine
The engine is between the wheels of a bike, and normally drives the back wheel with a chain. The higher the cc rating of the engine, the more powerful the bike will be.

Exhaust
A pipe at the back of a vehicle, through which waste gas and liquid produced by the cylinder of the engine escapes.

Freestyle
A stunt competition in which the rider can choose the movements that are performed.

FMX Freestyle Motocross
A combination of Motocross racing and Freestyle stunts.

Leathers
Clothing made from leather which is designed to protect the rider if there is an accident.

Motocross
Racing held on mud tracks. It is also known as MX or dirt bike racing.

Name tag
An identification tag worn by a motorbike racer so that medical teams will know the person's identity immediately if there is a crash.

Pits
An area at the side of the track where mechanics work on the bikes.

Ramp
A high platform, made of wood or metal or just piled earth, used for making jumps.

Shock absorbers

Part of the suspension of a bike or other vehicle that helps to smooth out the bumps and jumps.

Sidecar

Name used for a racing vehicle that is a combination of a motorbike and a sidecar.

Speedway

Motorbike racing in which the competitors race around a track using lightweight bikes with no brakes and no suspension.

Sponsor

A person or company who pays a team or rider's expenses, often for advertising purposes.

Superbike

A fast, powerful bike modified from a model on sale to the public.

Supermoto

A cross between freestyle motorcycling and motocross, which has track and cross-country sections.

Suspension

The system that supports the body of a bike or other vehicle on the wheel axles.

TT Tourist Trophy

A road race that has been held on the Isle of Man every year since 1907.

Tread

The raised pattern on a tyre which helps it to grip the surface of the track. It also channels away rainwater so the tyre does not slip in the wet. Off-road bikes use tyres with a deep-cut square pattern of squares.

Visor

A transparent protective shield that is attached to a bike helmet and pulls down to protect the eyes.

Index

A
acceleration 9, 30
accidents 17, 18, 22–23, 24, 26
aerodynamics 20, 30
Agostini, Giacomo 10

B
backflips 16
Barros, Alex 10, 13
Biaggi, Max 10–11
boots 6
brakes 18

C
Capes, Ryan 16
Capirossi, Loris 12
cc (cubic centimetres) 4, 10–12, 20
chassis 20, 30
Chevalier, M. 4
clothing 6–7
Clowers, Tommy 17
corners 5, 12, 18, 20
cubic centimetres see cc
cylinders 4, 10–11

D
dashboard 5
dirt bike racing see motocross
Doohan, Mick 24

E
Edwards, Colin 10
engines 4, 9, 10–11, 14, 20, 30
Evel Knievel 17
exhaust 8, 30

F
first race 4
`flip the bike' 22
FMX see Freestyle Motocross
foam pits 16
freestyle 5, 30
freestyle motocross (FMX) 16–17

G
gearbox 4
gloves 6
Grand Prix 26, 28–9

H
Haga, Noriyuki 14, 24
Hayden, Nicky 10, 15
Hayden, Roger and Tommy 15
helmets 6–7
heroes 24–25
Hopkins, John 9

I
Isle of Mann Tourist Trophy 22, 29

J
jumps 8, 16–17

K
Kato, Dajiro 23
Kazama, Shinji 27
knee guards 6–7

L
Laconi, Regis 14
leathers 6–7, 30
Lougher, Ian 22

M
McGregor, Ewan 7
map 28–29
mechanics 12, 18
medical teams 6, 22
mental preparation 22, 26
mini-bike races 9
motocross (MX) 4–5, 8–9,
     26, 30
MotoGP 4–5, 10–13,
28–29
Motorcycle Grand Prix
see motoGP
MX see motocross

N
name tags 6, 30
Noonan, John 24

P
pedals 8
pistons 4
pits 18, 30
protective clothing 6–7

R
race tracks 8, 12–15, 19
ramps 16–17, 30
records 10, 24
Reeves, Tim and Tristan 20
Rikkardson, Tony 25
risks 22–23
Roberts, Kenny 10, 24–25
Roberts, Kenny Jr 25
Roper, Sylvester Howard 4
Rossi, Valentino 10, 24, 27

S
safety 6–7
shock absorbers 8, 31
sidecars 4, 20–21, 31
speed records 10, 24
speeds 4, 12–13, 16
speedway 4, 18–19, 26, 31

sponsors 12, 31
`squids' 26
steering 18
stunts 16–17
superbikes 5, 14–15, 26–27, 31
supercross 8
supermoto 8, 31
Surtees, John 25
suspension 18, 31

T
tabletop 17
teams 12, 14
Toseland, James 14
Tourist Trophy (TT) 22, 31
tracks 8, 12–15, 19
tread 9, 31
TT see Tourist Trophy
tyres 9, 20

V
visors 6, 31

W
Webster, Steve 21
wet weather 23
Woodhead, Paul 21
World Champions 10–11
World Championships 14, 20,
     24–25, 28–29